Broadway's Memorable Melodies

A DIRECTORY OF THE POPULAR SONGS FROM THE MUSICAL THEATRE

Compiled by
ALVIN SCHULTZBERG

The Town House Press / Pittsboro, North Carolina

Library of Congress Number:95-61434
International Standard Book Number: 0-940653-41-9

Printed in the United States of America

Published by

The Town House Press, Inc.
552 Fearrington Post
Pittsboro NC 27312

℘

Publisher's Note: All proceeds from the sale of this book
will be distributed among various organizations
dedicated to cancer research.

Dedication

To my wife, Fran, whose musical talent
was relegated to singing in the shower
when no one else was around, but
forgave and encouraged me anyway.

Acknowledgments

I am indebted to Bill Blacher, neighbor, friend, and skilled musician, who got me started on this project by lending me a book.

And to Stanley Green, author of *The World of Musical Comedy*, which is the name of the book Bill Blacher lent me...and provided me with much of the reference material for this directory.

And finally, I am indebted to Bill Gates, who produced the Microsoft Windows program that allowed my PC to reduce the transcription time on this directory to a couple of months, instead of 200 years.

SOURCES:

The World of Musical Comedy by Stanley Green (A.S. Barnes and Company, 1967); *Popular American Composers* by David Ewin (H.W. Wilson, 1972); *Show Tunes* by Steven Suskin (Dodd-Mead, 1986); *Penquin Encyclopedia of Popular Music* by Donald Clarke, ed. (Viking Press, 1989); *Bakers Biographical Dictionary of Musicians* by Nicolas Slonimsky (Shirmer Books, 1992); *Guinness Encyclopedia of Popular Music* by Colin Larkin, ed. (Guinness Publishing Ltd, 1992). *Encyclopedia of Theatre Music* by Richard Lewine & Alfred Simon (Random House, 1961)

PHOTO CREDITS:
Page 2: Irving Berlin: *Courtesy Irving Berlin*, The Gershwins: *Gerswin Archives*.
Page 40: Lerner and Loewe: *Karsh;* Cole Porter: *Leo Friedman*, Kern and Hammerstein: *Vandamm*.
Page 74: Styne, Comden and Green: *ASCAP*. Sigmund Romberg: *N.Y. Public Library*, Henderson, DeSylva and Brown: *Max Munn Autrey*.
Page 96: Victor Herbert: *ASCAP*. Bock and Harnick: *Friedman-Abeles*.

A Foreword

This is a "fun" book. How does a directory with nothing but names and dates become fun? It depends on how you look at it.

Music has always been one of my interests, and particularly popular music -- what singers and band leaders call "standards." These are the songs sung by night club headliners and television guest stars, played by dance orchestras and concert bands, and hummed by people like you and me.

Over the years, three major sources produced America's popular melodies: sheet music (records and CD's later on), Hollywood films, and the musical theatre -- which is vaguely dubbed "Broadway." Why Broadway? Because a theatre production is usually deemed successful if it gets to the Great White Way ...and stays there a while.*

This directory deals with those melodies created for the Broadway stage. Not that I don't enjoy other sources of popular music. The music industry of Tin Pan Alley reigned supreme during the early part of this century, catering to the varied tastes of the public. And for more than three decades the great Hollywood musicals kept the country tapping its toes to songs from films like *Born to Dance (1936)*, *State Fair (1945)*, *High Society (1956)*, and *Gigi (1958)*.

But strangely, Hollywood's most prolific song-writers never became household names like their Broadway counterparts. For instance,

---

* *The Fantasticks* was a major exception. It opened off-Broadway and stayed there with more than 700 performances -- and countless road companies.

Harry Warren wrote "I Gotta Gal in Kalamazoo", "You"ll Never Know" and "Lullaby of Broadway", but the public hardly remembers him.

By contrast, the more renowned of the Hollywood composers and lyricists first found fame in the theatre and then moved on to song writing for the movies during their creative careers. Jerome Kern and George Gershwin, for example, shared time successfully on both coasts.

The basis for my *Broadway's Memorable Melodies* is the body of songs from people like Kern and Gershwin and Cole Porter and Richard Rodgers...along with 163 other composers and lyricists who wrote for the theatre. To me, there is something special about Broadway's melodies. Written to set the mood of the show, or to move the story along, they are created to appeal to sophisticated (and highly critical) audiences. The emphasis in this book, however, is on the most *memorable* of those melodies.

What makes them memorable? Their durability. If a song continues to be sung or played publicly, it qualifies for inclusion. Not every show tune becomes popular, despite the smashing success of the show itself. Andrew Lloyd Webber presented *Evita* in opera form -- the entire libretto was sung. Yet we would be hard pressed to remember a single melody except for "Don't Cry for Me, Argentina."

If this directory were all about the shows, and not about the melodies, it would have been gratifying to include every long-running show that ever hit Broadway. But since only those with at least one memorable melody are listed, Charles Strouse's *Golden Boy* (starring Sammy Davis, Jr.) is omitted, even though it ran for 509 performances.

On the other hand, enduring shows like *West Side Story, My Fair Lady,* and *The Sound of Music* each produced at least eight wonderfully popular songs that most people remember and can recognize.*

Herein lies the purpose of this directory...and also the "fun" of it. Call it a nostalgia nudge, or a trivia travel-guide, but everyone who enjoys popular music has wracked his or her brain trying to remember who wrote a familiar song, or what show it came from, or when they first heard it.

I have distilled the entire production of musical theatre melodies written from 1891 to 1988 to a total figure of 587 that I consider memorable. I am sure that other devotees might want to add to the list (hopefully with difficulty). Some might say that there are too many.

For example, the novelty patter song from Cole Porter's *DuBarry Was a Lady* called "Did You Evah" would only be included by those of us who connect it with comedian Bert Lahr. So if you don't remember Bert (the cowardly lion in *The Wizard of Oz*), you probably won't consider "Did You Evah" memorable.

Also, the songs of Alexander Borodin and Edvard Grieg might be considered "ringers" to some. Let me try to qualify. These are the only classical composers included--and for good reason. The melodies from the

---

* The reader will be disappointed that George and Ira Gershwin's immortal "The Man I Love" does not appear in the listings in this book. The number was dropped before the Broadway opening of *Lady Be Good* in 1926, because Adele Astaire did not have the voice to carry the song properly. Sheet music and recordings accounted for its phenomenal success.

Broadway shows *Kismet* and *The Song of Norway* were based on their respective 19th-century compositions, but with the music adapted and the lyrics re-written to turn them into the form and substance of 20th-century American musical theatre.

In effect, Broadway *is* American musical theatre, despite its early beginnings when it was primarily a carry-over of European operetta. Victor Herbert, Rudolf Friml and Sigmund Romberg were born in Europe and brought that genre to the American stage. But by 1920, the musical theatre as we know it was all ours -- and Europe would only copy.

I have enjoyed putting this directory together. I hope, dear reader, that you will enjoy the fun of using it.

A.S.

Postscript:

After completing the four sections of this book--devoted exclusively to Broadway melodies--I could not resist the urge to add an appendix that would include the memorable music that these Broadway composers created for the movies. It is a tribute to the diversity of their talents that must not be ignored.

November 1995
Fearrington Village, North Carolina

Contents

Section One

♉

Song Titles
(Alphabetically Listed)

BROADWAY'S LEADING COMPOSERS

← RICHARD RODGERS (right) and lyri LORENZ HART, his collaborator fron 1924 to 1942.

IRVING BERLIN, dressed for a singing role in the production of *This Is The Army* (1942). →

GEORGE GERSHWIN (right) and brother IRA, teamed together from 1922 until George's death in 1937. ↓

After the Ball
Music by: Percy Gaunt
Lyrics by: Charles Harris
Show: A Trip to Chinatown
Opening: November 1891

Ah! Sweet Mystery of Life
Music by: Victor Herbert
Lyrics by: Rida Johnson Young
Show: Naughty Marietta
Opening: November 1910

Alice Blue Gown
Music by: Harry Tierney
Lyrics by: Joseph McCarthy
Show: Irene
Opening: November 1919

All at Once
Music by: Richard Rodgers
Lyrics by: Lorenz Hart
Show: Babes in Arms
Opening: April 1937

All At Once You Love Her
Music by: Richard Rodgers
Lyrics by: Oscar Hammerstein II
Show: Pipe Dream
Opening: November 1955

All er Nothin'
Music by: Richard Rodgers
Lyrics by: Oscar Hammerstein II
Show: Oklahoma!
Opening: March 1943

All I Need is the Girl
Music by: Jule Styne
Lyrics by: Stephen Sondheim
Show: Gypsy
Opening: May 1959

All in Fun
Music by: Jerome Kern
Lyrics by: Oscar Hammerstein II
Show: Very Warm for May
Opening: November 1939

All the Things You Are
Music by: Jerome Kern
Lyrics by: Oscar Hammerstein II
Show: Very Warm for May
Opening: November 1939

All Through the Night
Music by: Cole Porter
Lyrics by: Cole Porter
Show: Anything Goes
Opening: November 1934

Almost Like Being in Love
Music by: Frederick Loewe
Lyrics by: Alan Jay Lerner
Show: Brigadoon
Opening: March 1947

Alone Together
Music by: Arthur Schwartz
Lyrics by: Howard Dietz
Show: Flying Colors
Opening: September 1932

Always True to You in My Fashion
Music by: Cole Porter
Lyrics by: Cole Porter
Show: Kiss Me Kate
Opening: December 1940

America
Music by: Leonard Bernstein
Lyrics by: Stephen Sondheim
Show: West Side Story
Opening: September 1957

American Eagles
Music by: Irving Berlin
Lyrics by: Irving Berlin
Show: This is the Army
Opening: July 1942

And This is My Beloved
Music by: Alexander Borodin
Lyrics by: Robert Wright &
George Forrest
Show: Kismet
Opening: December 1953

Another Op'nin, Another Show
Music by: Cole Porter
Lyrics by: Cole Porter
Show: Kiss Me Kate
Opening: December 1940

Anything Goes
Music by: Cole Porter
Lyrics by: Cole Porter
Show: Anything Goes
Opening: November 1934

Anything You Can Do
Music by: Irving Berlin
Lyrics by: Irving Berlin
Show: Annie Get Your Gun
Opening: May 1946

April in Paris
Music by: Vernon Duke
Lyrics by: E.Y. Harburg
Show: Walk a Little Faster
Opening: December 1932

April Showers
Music by: Louis Silvers
Lyrics by: B.G. DeSylva
Show: Bombo
Opening: October 1921

Aquarius
Music by: Galt MacDermot
Lyrics by: Gerome Ragni & James Rado
Show: Hair
Opening: April 1968

As Long As He Needs Me
Music by: Lionel Bart
Lyrics by: Lionel Bart
Show: Oliver!
Opening: January 1963

At Long Last Love
Music by: Cole Porter
Lyrics by: Cole Porter
Show: You Never Know
Opening: September 1938

Auf Wiedersehn
Music by: Sigmund Romberg
Lyrics by: Herbert Reynolds
Show: Blue Paradise
Opening: August 1915

Bali Ha'i
Music by: Richard Rodgers
Lyrics by: Oscar Hammerstein
Show: South Pacific
Opening: April 1949

Ballad of Mack the Knife, The
Music by: Kurt Weill
Lyrics by: Marc Blitstein
Show: Three-Penny Opera
Opening: March 1954

Baubles, Bangles and Beads
Music by: Alexander Borodin
Lyrics by: Robert Wright & George
Forrest
Show: Kismet
Opening: December 1953

Be a Santa
Music by: Jule Styne
Lyrics by: Adolph Green & Betty
Comden
Show: Subways Are For Sleeping
Opening: December 1961

Because You're You
Music by: Victor Herbert
Lyrics by: Henry Blossom
Show: Red Mill
Opening: September 1906

Begin the Beguine
Music by: Cole Porter
Lyrics by: Cole Porter
Show: Jubilee
Opening: October 1935

Bess, You is My Woman Now
Music by: George Gershwin
Lyrics by: Ira Gershwin
Show: Porgy and Bess
Opening: October 1935

Best of Times, The
Music by: Jerry Herman
Lyrics by: Harvey Fierstein
Show: La Cage Aux Folles
Opening: August 1983

Best Thing for You, The
Music by: Irving Berlin
Lyrics by: Irving Berlin
Show: Call Me Madam
Opening: October 1950

Best Things in Life Are Free, The
Music by: Ray Henderson
Lyrics by: B.G. DeSylva and Lew Brown
Show: Good News!
Opening: September 1927

Bewitched, Bothered and Bewildered
Music by: Richard Rodgers
Lyrics by: Lorenz Hart
Show: Pal Joey
Opening: December 1940

Bianca
Music by: Cole Porter
Lyrics by: Cole Porter
Show: Kiss Me Kate
Opening: December 1940

Bidin' My Time
Music by: George Gershwin
Lyrics by: Ira Gershwin
Show: Girl Crazy
Opening: October 1930

Big "D"
Music by: Frank Loesser
Lyrics by: Frank Loesser
Show: Most Happy Fella
Opening: May 1956

Big Spender
Music by: Cy Coleman
Lyrics by: Dorothy Fields
Show: Sweet Charity
Opening: January 1966

Bill
Music by: Jerome Kern
Lyrics by: Oscar Hammerstein II &
P.G. Wodehouse
Show: Showboat
Opening: December 1927

Birth of the Blues
Music by: Ray Henderson
Lyrics by: B.G. DeSylva and Lew Brown
Show: George White's Scandals (8th Edition)
Opening: June 1926

Black Bottom
Music by: Ray Henderson
Lyrics by: B.G. DeSylva and Lew Brown
Show: George White's Scandals (8th Edition)
Opening: June 1926

Bloody Mary
Music by: Richard Rodgers
Lyrics by: Oscar Hammerstein
Show: South Pacific
Opening: April 1949

Blow, Gabriel, Blow
Music by: Cole Porter
Lyrics by: Cole Porter
Show: Anything Goes
Opening: November 1934

The Blue Room
Music by: Richard Rodgers
Lyrics by: Lorenz Hart
Show: The Girl Friend
Opening: March 1926

Blue Skies
Music by: Irving Berlin
Lyrics by: Irving Berlin
Show: Betsy
Opening: December 1926

Bowery, The
Music by: Percy Gaunt
Lyrics by: Percy Gaunt
Show: A Trip to Chinatown
Opening: November 1891

Brother Can You Spare a Dime?
Music by: Jay Gorney
Lyrics by: E.Y. Harburg
Show: Americana
Opening: October 1932

Brotherhood of Man
Music by: Frank Loesser
Lyrics by: Frank Loesser
Show: How to Succeed in Business
        Without Really Trying
Opening: October 1961

Brush Up Your Shakespeare
Music by: Cole Porter
Lyrics by: Cole Porter
Show: Kiss Me Kate
Opening: December 1940

Buckle Down Winsocki
Music by: Hugh Martin
Lyrics by: Ralph Blane
Show: Best Foot Forward
Opening: October 1941

Bushel and a Peck
Music by: Frank Loesser
Lyrics by: Frank Loesser
Show: Guys and Dolls
Opening: November 1950

But Not for Me
Music by: George Gershwin
Lyrics by: Ira Gershwin
Show: Girl Crazy
Opening: October 1930

Button Up Your Overcoat
Music by: Ray Henderson
Lyrics by: B.G. DeSylva and Lew Brown
Show: Follow Thru
Opening: January 1929

Bye, Bye, Baby
Music by: Jule Styne
Lyrics by: Leo Robin
Show: Gentlemen Prefer Blondes
Opening: December 1949

C'est Magnifique
Music by: Cole Porter
Lyrics by: Cole Porter
Show: Can-Can
Opening: May 1953

Cabaret
Music by: John Kander
Lyrics by: Fred Ebb
Show: Cabaret
Opening: November 1966

Cabin in the Sky
Music by: Vernon Duke
Lyrics by: John Latouche
Show: Cabin in the Sky
Opening: October 1940

Camelot
Music by: Frederick Loewe
Lyrics by: Alan Jay Lerner
Show: Camelot
Opening: December 1960

Can't Help Lovin' Dat Man
Music by: Jerome Kern
Lyrics by: Oscar Hammerstein II
Show: Showboat
Opening: December 1927

Clap Yo' Hands
Music by: George Gershwin
Lyrics by: Ira Gershwin
Show: Oh, Kay!
Opening: November 1926

Climb Ev'ry Mountain
Music by: Richard Rodgers
Lyrics by: Oscar Hammerstein II
Show: Sound of Music
Opening: November 1959

Cloe
Music by: B.G. DeSylva
Lyrics by: B.G. DeSylva
Show: Sinbad
Opening: February 1918

Close As Pages in a Book
Music by: Sigmund Romberg
Lyrics by: Dorothy Fields
Show: Up in Central Park
Opening: January 1945

Cockeyed Optimist, A
Music by: Richard Rodgers
Lyrics by: Oscar Hammerstein
Show: South Pacific
Opening: April 1949

Come Rain or Come Shine
Music by: Harold Arlen
Lyrics by: Johnny Mercer
Show: St. Louis Woman
Opening: March 1946

Come to Me, Bend to Me
Music by: Frederick Loewe
Lyrics by: Alan Jay Lerner
Show: Brigadoon
Opening: March 1947

Comedy Tonight
Music by: Stephen Sondheim
Lyrics by: Stephen Sondheim
Show: Funny Thing Happened on the
Way to the Forum
Opening: May 1962

Comes Love
Music by: Sam Stept
Lyrics by: Lew Brown & Charles Tobias
Show: Yokel Boy
Opening: July 1939

Comes Once in a Lifetime
Music by: Jule Styne
Lyrics by: Adolph Green & Betty Comden
Show: Subways Are For Sleeping
Opening: December 1961

Company Way
Music by: Frank Loesser
Lyrics by: Frank Loesser
Show: How to Succeed in Business
Without Really Trying
Opening: October 1961

Cool
Music by: Leonard Bernstein
Lyrics by: Stephen Sondheim
Show: West Side Story
Opening: September 1957

Could You Use Me?
Music by: George Gershwin
Lyrics by: Ira Gershwin
Show: Girl Crazy
Opening: October 1930

Cry Like the Wind
Music by: Jule Styne
Lyrics by: Adolph Green & Betty
Comden
Show: Do Re Mi
Opening: December 1960

Cuddle Up a Little Closer Lovey Mine
Music by: Karl Hoschna
Lyrics by: Otto Harbach
Show: Three Twins
Opening: June 1908

Dancing in the Dark
Music by: Arthur Schwartz
Lyrics by: Howard Dietz
Show: Band Wagon
Opening: June 1931

Day by Day
Music by: Stephen Schwartz
Lyrics by: John-Michael Tebelak
Show: Godspell
Opening: May 1971

Deep in My Heart
Music by: Vincent Youmans
Lyrics by: Zelda Sears
Show: Lollipop
Opening: January 1924

Deep in My Heart Dear
Music by: Sigmund Romberg
Lyrics by: Dorothy Donnelly
Show: Student Prince in Heidelberg
Opening: December 1924

Desert Song
Music by: Sigmund Romberg
Lyrics by: Otto Harbach & Oscar
　　　　　　Hammerstein II
Show: Desert Song
Opening: November 1926

Diamonds Are a Girl's Best Friend
Music by: Jule Styne
Lyrics by: Leo Robin
Show: Gentlemen Prefer Blondes
Opening: December 1949

Diga Diga Doo
Music by: Jimmy McHugh
Lyrics by: Dorothy Fields
Show: Blackbirds of 1928
Opening: May 1928

Dîtes-Moi
Music by: Richard Rodgers
Lyrics by: Oscar Hammerstein II
Show: South Pacific
Opening: April 1949

Do I Hear a Waltz?
Music by: Richard Rodgers
Lyrics by: Stephen Sondheim
Show: Do I Hear a Waltz?
Opening: March 1965

Do I Love You?
Music by: Cole Porter
Lyrics by: Cole Porter
Show: Dubarry Was a Lady
Opening: December 1939

Do-Re-Mi
Music by: Richard Rodgers
Lyrics by: Oscar Hammerstein II
Show: Sound of Music
Opening: November 1959

Doin' What Comes Natur'lly
Music by: Irving Berlin
Lyrics by: Irving Berlin
Show: Annie Get Your Gun
Opening: May 1946

Don't Cry for Me, Argentina
Music by: Andrew Lloyd Webber
Lyrics by: Tim Rice
Show: Evita
Opening: September 1979

Don't Ever Leave Me
Music by: Jerome Kern
Lyrics by: Oscar Hammerstein II
Show: Sweet Adeline
Opening: September 1929

Don't Rain on My Parade
Music by: Jule Styne
Lyrics by: Bob Merrill
Show: Funny Girl
Opening: March 1964

Drinking Song
Music by: Sigmund Romberg
Lyrics by: Dorothy Donnelly
Show: Student Prince in Heidelberg
Opening: December 1924

Drums in My Heart
Music by: Vincent Youmans
Lyrics by: Edward Heyman
Show: Through the Years
Opening: January 1932

Eadie Was a Lady
Music by: Richard A. Whiting
Lyrics by: B.G. DeSylva
Show: Take a Chance
Opening: Novermber 1932

Eagle and Me, The
Music by: Harold Arlen
Lyrics by: E.Y. Harburg
Show: Bloomer Girl
Opening: October 1944

Easter Parade
Music by: Irving Berlin
Lyrics by: Irving Berlin
Show: As Thousands Cheer
Opening: September 1933

Edelweiss
Music by: Richard Rodgers
Lyrics by: Oscar Hammerstein II
Show: Sound of Music
Opening: November 1959

Embraceable You
Music by: George Gershwin
Lyrics by: Ira Gershwin
Show: Girl Crazy
Opening: October 1930

Ev'rytime We Say Goodbye
Music by: Cole Porter
Lyrics by: Cole Porter
Show: Seven Lively Arts
Opening: December 1944

Every Day is Ladies' Day with Me
Music by: Victor Herbert
Lyrics by: Henry Blossom
Show: Red Mill
Opening: September 1906

Every Little Movement
Music by: Karl Hoschna
Lyrics by: Otto Harbach
Show: Madame Sherry
Opening: August 1910

Everything's Coming Up Roses
Music by: Jule Styne
Lyrics by: Stephen Sondheim
Show: Gypsy
Opening: May 1959

Exactly Like You
Music by: Jimmy McHugh
Lyrics by: Dorothy Fields
Show: International Revue
Opening: February 1930

F.D.R. Jones
Music by: Harold Rome
Lyrics by: Harold Rome
Show: Sing Out the News
Opening: September 1928

Falling in Love With Love
Music by: Richard Rodgers
Lyrics by: Lorenz Hart
Show: Boys from Syacuse
Opening: November 1938

Fanny
Music by: Harold Rome
Lyrics by: Harold Rome
Show: Fanny
Opening: November 1954

Fascinating Rhythm
Music by: George Gershwin
Lyrics by: Ira Gershwin
Show: Lady, Be Good!
Opening: December 1924

Feeling I'm Falling
Music by: George Gershwin
Lyrics by: Ira Gershwin
Show: Strike Up the Band
Opening: November 1928

Fellow Needs a Girl, A
Music by: Richard Rodgers
Lyrics by: Oscar Hammerstein II
Show: Allegro
Opening: October 1947

Fine and Dandy
Music by: Kay Swift
Lyrics by: Paul James
Show: Fine and Dandy
Opening: September 1930

Follow Me
Music by: Frederick Loewe
Lyrics by: *Alan* Jay Lerner
Show: Camelot
Opening: December 1960

Fools Fall in Love
Music by: Irving Berlin
Lyrics by: Irving Berlin
Show: Louisiana Purchase
Opening: May 1940

Forty-Five Minutes from Broadway
Music by: George M. Cohan
Lyrics by: George M. Cohan
Show: Forty-Five Minutes from Broadway
Opening: January 1906

Freddy and His Fiddle
Music by: Edvard Grieg
Lyrics by: Robert Wright & George
           Forrest
Show: Song of Norway
Opening: August 1944

Freedom
Music by: Gary Geld
Lyrics by: Peter Udell
Show: Shenandoah
Opening: January 1975

Friendship
Music by: Cole Porter
Lyrics by: Cole Porter
Show: Dubarry Was a Lady
Opening: December 1939

Funny Face
Music by: George Gershwin
Lyrics by: Ira Gershwin
Show: Funny Face
Opening: November 1927

Gee, Officer Krupke
Music by: Leonard Bernstein
Lyrics by: Stephen Sondheim
Show: West Side Story
Opening: September 1957

Gentleman is a Dope, The
Music by: Richard Rodgers
Lyrics by: Oscar Hammerstein II
Show: Allegro
Opening: October 1947

Get Me to the Church on Time
Music by: Frederick Loewe
Lyrics by: Alan Jay Lerner
Show: My Fair Lady
Opening: March 1956

Get Out of Town
Music by: Cole Porter
Lyrics by: Cole Porter
Show: Leave It to Me
Opening: November 1938

Getting to Know You
Music by: Richard Rodgers
Lyrics by: Oscar Hammerstein II
Show: King and I
Opening: March 1951

Giannina Mia
Music by: Rudolf Friml
Lyrics by: Otto Harbach
Show: Firefly
Opening: December 1912

Girl Friend, The
Music by: Richard Rodgers
Lyrics by: Lorenz Hart
Show: The Girl Friend
Opening: March 1926

Girl of My Dreams
Music by: Karl Hoschna
Lyrics by: Otto Harbach
Show: Girl of My Dreams
Opening: August 1911

Girl That I Marry, The
Music by: Irving Berlin
Lyrics by: Irving Berlin
Show: Annie Get Your Gun
Opening: May 1946

Give My Regards to Broadway
Music by: George M. Cohan
Lyrics by: George M. Cohan .
Show: Little Johnny Jones
Opening: November 1904

Golden Days
Music by: Sigmund Romberg
Lyrics by: Dorothy Donnelly
Show: Student Prince in Heidelberg
Opening: December 1924

Gonna Build a Mountain
Music by: Anthony Newley
Lyrics by: Leslie Bricusse
Show: Stop the World -- I Want to Get Off
Opening: October 1962

Good News
Music by: Ray Henderson
Lyrics by: B.G. DeSylva and Lew Brown
Show: Good News!
Opening: September 1927

Good Night, Sweetheart
Music by: Ray Noble
Lyrics by: Peg Connelly
Show: Earl Carroll Vanities
Opening: August 1927

Goodnight, My Someone
Music by: Meredith Willson
Lyrics by: Meredith Willson
Show: Music Man
Opening: December 1957

Great Day
Music by: Vincent Youmans
Lyrics by: Billy Rose and Edward Eliscu
Show: Great Day!
Opening: October 1929

Green-Up Time
Music by: Kurt Weill
Lyrics by: Alan Jay Lerner
Show: Lovelife
Opening: October 1948

Guys and Dolls
Music by: Frank Loesser
Lyrics by: Frank Loesser
Show: Guys and Dolls
Opening: November 1950

Gypsy Love Song
Music by: Victor Herbert
Lyrics by: Harry B.Smith
Show: Fortune Teller
Opening: September 1928

Hallelujah
Music by: Vincent Youmans
Lyrics by: Clifford Grey & Leo
Robbins
Show: Hit the Deck
Opening: April 1927

Happy Talk
Music by: Richard Rodgers
Lyrics by: Oscar Hammerstein II
Show: South Pacific
Opening: April 1949

Harrigan
Music by: George M. Cohan
Lyrics by: George M. Cohan
Show: Fifty Miles from Boston
Opening: February 1908

Have I Told You Lately?
Music by: Harold Rome
Lyrics by: Harold Rome
Show: I Can Get It For You
Wholesale
Opening: March 1962

Have You Met Miss Jones?
Music by: Richard Rodgers
Lyrics by: Lorenz Hart
Show: I'd Rather Be Right
Opening: November 1937

He Loves and She Loves
Music by: George Gershwin
Lyrics by: Ira Gershwin
Show: Funny Face
Opening: November 1927

Heart
Music by: Richard Adler
Lyrics by: Jerry Ross
Show: Damn Yankees
Opening: May 1955

Heat Wave
Music by: Irving Berlin
Lyrics by: Irving Berlin
Show: As Thousands Cheer
Opening: September 1933

Heather on the Hill
Music by: Frederick Loewe
Lyrics by: Alan Jay Lerner
Show: Brigadoon
Opening: March 1947

Hello, Dolly!
Music by: Jerry Herman
Lyrics by: Jerry Herman
Show: Hello, Dolly!
Opening: January 1964

Hello, Young Lovers
Music by: Richard Rodgers
Lyrics by: Oscar Hammerstein II
Show: King and I
Opening: March 1951

Here I'll Stay
Music by: Kurt Weill
Lyrics by: Alan Jay Lerner
Show: Lovelife
Opening: October 1948

Hernando's Hideaway
Music by: Richard Adler
Lyrics by: Jerry Ross
Show: Pajama Game
Opening: May 1954

Hey, There
Music by: Richard Adler
Lyrics by: Jerry Ross
Show: Pajama Game
Opening: May 1954

Hey, Look Me Over
Music by: Cy Coleman
Lyrics by: Carolyn Leigh
Show: Wildcat
Opening: December 1960

Hey, Good Lookin'
Music by: Cole Porter
Lyrics by: Cole Porter
Show: Something for the Boys
Opening: January 1943

Honey Bun
Music by: Richard Rodgers
Lyrics by: Oscar Hammerstein II
Show: South Pacific
Opening: April 1949

Hostess with the Mostes' on the Ball, The
Music by: Irving Berlin
Lyrics by: Irving Berlin
Show: Call Me Madam
Opening: October 1950

How Are Things in Glocca Morra?
Music by: Burton Lane
Lyrics by: E.Y. Harburg
Show: Finian's Rainbow
Opening: January 1947

How Do You Speak to an Angel?
Music by: Jule Styne
Lyrics by: Bob Hilliard
Show: Hazel Flagg
Opening: February 1953

How Long Has This Been Going On?
Music by: George Gershwin
Lyrics by: Ira Gershwin
Show: Rosalie
Opening: January 1928

How to Handle a Woman
Music by: Frederick Loewe
Lyrics by: Alan Jay Lerner
Show: Camelot
Opening: December 1960

I Ain't Down Yet
Music by: Meredith Willson
Lyrics by: Meredith Willson
Show: Insinkable Molly Brown
Opening: November 1960

I Believe in You
Music by: Frank Loesser
Lyrics by: Frank Loesser
Show: How to Succeed in Busines
Without Really Trying
Opening: October 1961

I Cain't Say No
Music by: Richard Rodgers
Lyrics by: Oscar Hammerstein II
Show: Oklahoma!
Opening: March 1943

I Can't Do the Sum
Music by: Victor Herbert
Lyrics by: Glen MacDonough
Show: Babes in Toyland
Opening: October 1903

I Can't Get Started
Music by: Vernon Duke
Lyrics by: E.Y. Harburg
Show: Ziegfeld Follies
Opening: January 1935

I Can't Give You Anything But Love
Music by: Jimmy McHugh
Lyrics by: Dorothy Fields
Show: Blackbirds of 1928
Opening: May 1928

I Could Have Danced All Night
Music by: Frederick Loewe
Lyrics by: Alan Jay Lerner
Show: My Fair Lady
Opening: March 1956

I Could Write a Book
Music by: Richard Rodgers
Lyrics by: Lorenz Hart
Show: Pal Joey
Opening: December 1940

I Didn't Know What Time It Was
Music by: Richard Rodgers
Lyrics by: Lorenz Hart
Show: Too Many Girls
Opening: October 1939

I Don't Know How to Love Him
Music by: Andrew Lloyd Webber
Lyrics by: Tim Rice
Show: Jesus Christ Superstar
Opening: October 1971

I Enjoy Being a Girl
Music by: Richard Rodgers
Lyrics by: Oscar Hammerstein II
Show: Flower Drum Song
Opening: December 1958

I Feel Pretty
Music by: Leonard Bernstein
Lyrics by: Stephen Sondheim
Show: West Side Story
Opening: September 1957

I Get a Kick Out of You
Music by: Cole Porter
Lyrics by: Cole Porter
Show: Anything Goes
Opening: November 1934

I Got Lost in His Arms
Music by: Irving Berlin
Lyrics by: Irving Berlin
Show: Annie Get Your Gun
Opening: May 1946

I Got Plenty of Nothin'
Music by: George Gershwin
Lyrics by: DuBose Heyward &
Ira Gershwin
Show: Porgy and Bess
Opening: October 1935

I Got Rythm
Music by: George Gershwin
Lyrics by: Ira Gershwin
Show: Girl Crazy
Opening: October 1930

I Got the Sun in the Morning
Music by: Irving Berlin
Lyrics by: Irving Berlin
Show: Annie Get Your Gun
Opening: May 1946

I Gotta Crow
Music by: Mark Sharlap
Lyrics by: Carolyn Leigh
Show: Peter Pan
Opening: Octrober 1954

I Guess I'll Have to Change My Plans
Music by: Arthur Schwartz
Lyrics by: Howard Dietz
Show: Little Show
Opening: April 1929

I Have Dreamed
Music by: Richard Rodgers
Lyrics by: Oscar Hammerstein II
Show: King and I
Opening: March 1951

I Know That You Know
Music by: Vincent Youmans
Lyrics by: Anne Caldwell
Show: Oh, Please!
Opening: December 1926

I Left My Heart at the Stage Door Canteen
Music by: Irving Berlin
Lyrics by: irving Berlin
Show: This is the Army
Opening: July 1942

I Like the Likes of You
Music by: Vernon Duke
Lyrics by: E.Y. Harburg
Show: Ziegfeld Follies
Opening: January 1934

I Like to Recognize the Tune
Music by: Richard Rodgers
Lyrics by: Lorenz Hart
Show: Too Many Girls
Opening: October 1939

I Love a Cop
Music by: Jerry Bock
Lyrics by: Sheldon Harnick
Show: Fiorello!
Opening: November 1959

I Love a Piano
Music by: Irving Berlin
Lyrics by: Irving Berlin
Show: Stop! Look! Listen!
Opening: December 1915

I Love Louisa
Music by: Arthur Schwartz
Lyrics by: Howard Dietz
Show: Band Wagon
Opening: Juen 1931

I Love Paris
Music by: Cokle Porter
Lyrics by: Cole Porter
Show: Can-Can
Opening: May 1953

I Love You
Music by: Edvard Grieg
Lyrics by: Robert Wright & George Forrest
Show: Song of Norway
Opening: August 1944

I Love You
Music by: Cole Porter
Lyrics by: Cole Porter
Show: Mexican Hayride
Opening: January 1944

I Loved You Once in Silence
Music by: Frederick Loewe
Lyrics by: Alan Jay Lerner
Show: Camelot
Opening: December 1960

I Loves You, Porgy
Music by: George Gershwin
Lyrics by: Ira Gershwin
Show: Porgy and Bess
Opening: October 1935

I Married an Angel
Music by: Richard Rodgers
Lyrics by: Lorenz Hart
Show: I Married an Angel
Opening: May 1938

I See Your Face Before Me
Music by: Arthur Schwartz
Lyrics by: Howard Dietz
Show: Between the Devil
Opening: December 1937

I Still Get Jealous
Music by: Jule Styne
Lyrics by: Sammy Cahn
Show: High Button Shoes
Opening: October 1947

I Talk to the Trees
Music by: Frederick Loewe
Lyrics by: Alan Jay Lerner
Show: Paint Your Wagon
Opening: November 1951

I Want to Be Happy
Music by: Vincent Youmans
Lyrics by: Irving Caesar
Show: No, No, Nanette
Opening: September 1925

I Want What I Want When I Want It
Music by: Victor Herbert
Lyrics by: Henry Blossom
Show: Mlle. Modiste
Opening: December 1905

I Whistle a Happy Tune
Music by: Richard Rodgers
Lyrics by: Oscar Hammerstein
Show: King and I
Opening: March 1951

I Wish I Were in Love Again
Music by: Richard Rodgers
Lyrics by: Lorenz Hart
Show: Babes in Arms
Opening: April 1937

I'd Do Anything
Music by: Lionel Bart
Lyrics by: Lionel Bart
Show: Oliver!
Opening: January 1963

I'll Build a Stairway to Paradise
Music by: George Gershwin
Lyrics by: B.G. DaSylva &
        Arthur Francis (Ira Gershwin)
Show: George White's Scandals
        (4th Edition)
Opening: August 1922

I'll Know
Music by: Frank Loesser
Lyrics by: Frank Loesser
Show: Guys and Dolls
Opening: November 1950

I'll Never Fall in Love Again
Music by: Burt Bacharach
Lyrics by: Hal David
Show: Promises, Promises
Opening: December 1968

I'll See You Again
Music by: Noël Coward
Lyrics by: Noël Coward
Show: Bitter Sweet
Opening: November 1929

I'm An Indian, Too
Music by: Irving Berlin
Lyrics by: Irving Berlin
Show: Annie Get Your Gun
Opening: May 1946

I'm Falling in Love with Someone
Music by: Victor Herbert
Lyrics by: Rida Johnson Young
Show: Naughty Marietta
Opening: November 1910

I'm Gonna Wash That Man Right Out of My Hair
Music by: Richard Rodgers
Lyrics by: Oscar Hammerstein II
Show: South Pacific
Opening: April 1949

I'm in Love Again
Music by: Cole Porter
Lyrics by: Cole Porter
Show: Greenwich Village Follies (6th Edition)
Opening: September 1924

I'm Just Wild About Harry
Music by: Eubie Blake
Lyrics by: Noble Sissle
Show: Shuffle Along
Opening: May 1921

I've Grown Accustomed to Her Face
Music by: Frederick Loewe
Lyrics by: Alan Jay Lerner
Show: My Fair Lady
Opening: March 1956

I've Got A Crush on You
Music by: George Gershwin
Lyrics by: Ira Gershwin
Show: Strike Up the Band
Opening: January 1930

I've Got Five Dollars
Music by: Richard Rodgers
Lyrics by: Lorenz Hart
Show: America's Sweetheart
Opening: February 1931

I've Never Been in Love Before
Music by: Frank Loesser
Lyrics by: Frank Loesser
Show: Guys and Dolls
Opening: November 1950

I've Told Every Little Star
Music by: Jerome Kern
Lyrics by: Oscar Hammerstein II
Show: Music in the Air
Opening: November 1932

If I Loved You
Music by: Richard Rodgers
Lyrics by: Oscar Hammerstein II
Show: Carousel
Opening: April 1945

If My Friends Could See Me Now
Music by: Cy Coleman
Lyrics by: Dorothy Fields
Show: Sweet Charity
Opening: January 1966

If Ever I Would Leave You
Music by: Frederick Loewe
Lyrics by: Alan Jay Lerner
Show: Camelot
Opening: December 1960

If He Walked Into My Life
Music by: Jerry Herman
Lyrics by: Jerry Herrnan
Show: Mame
Opening: May 1966

If I Were a Bell
Music by: Frank Loesser
Lyrics by: Frank Loesser
Show: Guys and Dolls
Opening: November 1950

If I Were a Rich Man
Music by: Jerry Bock
Lyrics by: Sheldon Harnick
Show: Fiddler on the Roof
Opening: September 1964

If There is Someone Lovelier Than You
Music by: Arthur Schwartz
Lyrics by: Howard Dietz
Show: Revenge with Music
Opening: November 1934

If This Isn't Love
Music by: Burton Lane
Lyrics by: E.Y. Harburg
Show: Finian's Rainbow
Opening: January 1947

If You Knew Susie
Music by: Joseph Meyer
Lyrics by: B.G. DeSylva
Show: Big Boy
Opening: January 1925

If You're In Love You'll Waltz
Music by: Harry Tierney
Lyrics by: Joseph McCarthy
Show: Rio Rita
Opening: Febrary 1927

Impossible Dream (The Quest)
Music by: Mitch Leigh
Lyrics by: Joe Darion
Show: Man of La Mancha
Opening: November 1965

Indian Love Call
Music by: Rudolf Friml
Lyrics by: Otto Harbach & Oscar
          Hammerstein II
Show: Rose-Marie
Opening: September 1924

Irene
Music by: Harry Tierney
Lyrics by: Joseph McCarthy
Show: Irene
Opening: November 1919

It Ain't Necessarily So
Music by: George Gershwin
Lyrics by: Ira Gershwin
Show: Porgy and Bess
Opening: October 1935

It All Depends on You
Music by: Ray Henderson
Lyrics by: Lew Brown
Show: Big Boy
Opening: January 1925

It Doesn't Cost You Anything to Dream
Music by: Sigmund Romberg
Lyrics by: Dorothy Fields
Show: Up in Central Park
Opening: January 1945

It Never Entered My Mind
Music by: Richard Rodgers
Lyrics by: Lorenz Hart
Show: Higher and Higher
Opening: April 1940

It Only Takes a Moment
Music by: Jerry Herman
Lyrics by: Jerry Herman
Show: Hello, Dolly!
Opening: January 1964

It's a Lovely Day Today
Music by: Irving Berlin
Lyrics by: Irving Berlin
Show: Call Me Madam
Opening: October 1950

It's a Lovely Day Tomorrow
Music by: Irving Berlin
Lyrics by: Irving Berlin
Show: Louisiana Purchase
Opening: May 1940

It's All Right with Me
Music by: Cole Porter
Lyrics by: Cole Porter
Show: Can-Can
Opening: May 1953

It's De-Lovely
Music by: Cole Porter
Lyrics by: Cole Porter
Show: Red, Hot and Blue!
Opening: October 1936

Johnny One Note
Music by: Richard Rodgers
Lyrics by: Lorenz Hart
Show: Babes in Arms
Opening: April 1937

June is Bustin' Out All Over
Music by: Richard Rodgers
Lyrics by: Oscar Hammerstein II
Show: Carousel
Opening: April 1945

Just in Time
Music by: Jule Styne
Lyrics by: Adoph Green & Betty
          Comden
Show: Bells are Ringing
Opening: November 1956

Just One of Those Things
Music by: Cole Porter
Lyrics by: Cole Porter
Show: Jubilee
Opening: October 1935

Just You Wait
Music by: Frederick Loewe
Lyrics by: Alan Jay Lerner
Show: My Fair Lady
Opening: March 1956

Kansas City
Music by: Richard Rodgers
Lyrics by: Oscar Hammerstein II
Show: Oklahoma!
Opening: March 1943

Kids
Music by: Charles Strouse
Lyrics by: Lee Adams
Show: Bye Bye Birdie
Opening: April 1960

Kinkajou, The
Music by: Harry Tierney
Lyrics by: Joseph McCarthy
Show: Rio Rita
Opening: Febrary 1927

Kiss in the Dark
Music by: Victor Herbert
Lyrics by: B.G.DeSylva
Show: Orange Blossoms
Opening: September 1922

Kiss Me Again
Music by: Victor Herbert
Lyrics by: Henry Blossom
Show: Mlle. Modiste
Opening: December 1905

Lady is a Tramp, The
Music by: Richard Rodgers
Lyrics by: Lorenz Hart
Show: Babes in Arms
Opening: April 1937

Lady of the Evening
Music by: Irving Berlin
Lyrics by: Irving Berlin
Show: Music Box Revue
Opening: October 1922

Learn to Croon
Music by: Harold Arlen
Lyrics by: Jack Yellen
Show: You Said It
Opening: January 1931

Let Me Entertain You
Music by: Jule Styne
Lyrics by: Stephen Sondheim
Show: Gypsy
Opening: May 1959

Let the Sunshine In
Music by: Galt MacDermot
Lyrics by: Gerome Ragni &
          James Rado
Show: Hair
Opening: April 1968

Let's Be Buddies
Music by: Cole Porter
Lyrics by: Cole Porter
Show: Panama Hattie
Opening: October 1940

Let's Do It
Music by: Cole Porter
Lyrics by: Cole Porter
Show: Paris
Opening: October 1928

**Let's Have Another Cup
o' Coffee**
Music by: Irving Berlin
Lyrics by: Irving Berlin
Show: Face the Music
Opening: February 1932

Let's Not Talk About Love
Music by: Cole Porter
Lyrics by: Cole Porter
Show: Let's Face It!
Opening: October 1941

Let's Take a Walk Around the Block
Music by: Harold Arlen
Lyrics by: E.Y. Harburg & Ira Gershwin
Show: Life Begins at 8:40
Opening: August 1934

Let's Take an Old Fashioned Walk
Music by: Irving Berlin
Lyrics by: Irving Berlin
Show: Miss Liberty
Opening: July 1949

Lida Rose
Music by: Meredith Willson
Lyrics by: Meredith Willson
Show: Music Man
Opening: December 1957

Life is Just a Bowl of Cherries
Music by: Ray Henderson
Lyrics by: Lew Brown
Show: George White's Scandals
        (11th Edition)
Opening: September 1931

Life Upon the Wicked Stage
Music by: Jerome Kern
Lyrics by: Oscar Hammerstein II
Show: Showboat
Opening: December 1927

Limehouse Blues
Music by: Philip Braham
Lyrics by: Douglas Furber
Show: Andre Charlot's Revue of 1924
Opening: January 1924

Little Girl Blue
Music by: Richard Rodgers
Lyrics by: Lorenz Hart
Show: Jumbo
Opening: November 1935

Little Lamb
Music by: Jule Styne
Lyrics by: Stephen Sondheim
Show: Gypsy
Opening: May 1959

Little Old Lady
Music by: Hoagy Carmichael
Lyrics by: Stanley Adams
Show: Show is On
Opening: December 1936

Little Tin Box
Music by: Jerry Bock
Lyrics by: Sheldon Harnick
Show: Fiorello!
Opening: November 1959

Liza
Music by: George Gershwin
Lyrics by: Ira Gershwin
Show: Show Girl
Opening: July 1929

Lonely Town
Music by: Leonard Bernstein
Lyrics by: Adolph Green & Betty
        Comden
Show: On the Town
Opening: December 1944

Look for the Silver Lining
Music by: Jerome Kern
Lyrics by: B.G. DeSylva
Show: Sally
Opening: December 1920

Look to the Rainbow
Music by: Burton Lane
Lyrics by: E.Y. Harburg
Show: Finian's Rainbow
Opening: January 1947

Lot of Livin' to Do, A
Music by: Charles Strouse
Lyrics by: Lee Adams
Show: Bye Bye Birdie
Opening: April 1960

Louisiana Hayride
Music by: Arthur Schwartz
Lyrics by: Howard Dietz
Show: Flying Colors
Opening: September 1932

Love, Look Away
Music by: Richard Rodgers
Lyrics by: Oscar Hammerstein II
Show: Flower Drum Song
Opening: December 1958

Love for Sale
Music by: Cole Porter
Lyrics by: Cole Porter
Show: New Yorkers
Opening: December 1930

Love is Like a Firefly
Music by: Rudolf Friml
Lyrics by: Otto Harbach
Show: Firefly
Opening: December 1912

Love is Sweeping the Country
Music by: George Gershwin
Lyrics by: Ira Gershwin
Show: Of Thee I Sing
Opening: December 1931

Love Makes the World Go Round
Music by: Bob Merrill
Lyrics by: Bob Merrill
Show: Carnival
Opening: April 1961

Love Me or Leave Me
Music by: Walter Donaldson
Lyrics by: Gus Kahn
Show: Whoopee
Opening: December 1928

Lover, Come Back to Me
Music by: Sigmund Romberg
Lyrics by: Oscar Hammerstein II
Show: New Moon
Opening: September 1928

Luck Be a Lady
Music by: Frank Loesser
Lyrics by: Frank Loesser
Show: Guys and Dolls
Opening: November 1950

Lucky in Love
Music by: Ray Henderson
Lyrics by: B.G. DeSylva and Lew Brown
Show: Good News!
Opening: September 1927

Make Believe
Music by: Jerome Kern
Lyrics by: Oscar Hammerstein II
Show: Showboat
Opening: December 1927

Make Our Garden Grow
Music by: Leonard Bernstein
Lyrics by: Richard Wilbur
Show: Candide
Opening: December 1956

Make Someone Happy
Music by: Jule Styne
Lyrics by: Adolph Green & Betty Comden
Show: Do Re Mi
Opening: December 1960

Makin' Whoopee
Music by: Walter Donaldson
Lyrics by: Gus Kahn
Show: Whoopee
Opening: December 1928

Mame
Music by: Jerry Herman
Lyrics by: Jerry Herman
Show: Mame
Opening: May 1966

Man of La Mancha (I, Don Quixote)
Music by: Jerry Leigh
Lyrics by: Joe Darion
Show: Man of La Mancha
Opening: November 1965

Mandy
Music by: Irving Berlin
Lyrics by: Irving Ber'in
Show: Yip, Yip, Yaphank
Opening: September 1918

Manhattan
Music by: Richard Rodgers
Lyrics by: Lorenz Hart
Show: Garrick Gaieties
Opening: May 1925

Many a New Day
Music by: Richard Rodgers
Lyrics by: Oscar Hammerstein II
Show: Oklahoma!
Opening: March 1943

March of the Toys
Music by: Victor Herbert
Lyrics by: Glen MacDonough
Show: Babes in Toyland
Opening: October 1903

Maria
Music by: Leonard Bernstein
Lyrics by: Stephen Sondheim
Show: West Side Story
Opening: September 1957

Maria
Music by: Richard Rodgers
Lyrics by: Oscar Hammerstein
Show: Sound of Music
Opening: November 1959

Marian the Librarian
Music by: Meredith Willson
Lyrics by: Meredith Willson
Show: Music Man
Opening: December 1957

Mary's a Grand Old Name
Music by: George M. Cohan
Lyrics by: George M. Cohan
Show: Forty-Five Minutes from Broadway
Opening: January 1906

Matchmaker, Matchmaker
Music by: Jerry Bock
Lyrics by: Sheldon Harnick
Show: Fiddler on the Roof
Opening: September 1964

Maybe
Music by: George Gershwin
Lyrics by: Ira Gershwin
Show: Oh, Kay!
Opening: November 1926

Memory
Music by: Andrew Lloyd Webber
Lyrics by: T.S. Eliot
Show: Cats
Opening: October 1982

Midsummer's Eve
Music by: Edvard Grieg
Lyrics by: Robert Wright & George
        Forrest
Show: Song of Norway
Opening: August 1944

Milk and Honey
Music by: Jerry Herman
Lyrics by: Jerry Herman
Show: Milk and Honey
Opening: October 1961

Miracle of Miracles
Music by: Jerry Bock
Lyrics by: Sheldon Harnick
Show: Fiddler on the Roof
Opening: September 1964

Molly Malone
Music by: George M. Cohan
Lyrics by: George M. Cohan
Show: Merry Malones
Opening: September 1927

More Than You Know
Music by: Vincent Youmans
Lyrics by: Billy Rose and
        Edward Eliscu
Show: Great Day!
Opening: October 1929

Most Beautiful Girl in the World, The
Music by: Richard Rodgers
Lyrics by: Lorenz Hart
Show: Jumbo
Opening: November 1935

Mountain Greenery
Music by: Richard Rodgers
Lyrics by: Lorenz Hart
Show: Garrick Gaieties
Opening: May 1926

Mr. Gallagher and Mr. Shean
Music by: Ed Gallagher
Lyrics by: Al Shean & Ernest Ball
Show: Ziegfeld Follies of 1922
Opening: June 1922

Mr. Snow
Music by: Richard Rodgers
Lyrics by: Oscar Hammerstein II
Show: Carousel
Opening: April 1945

Mr. Wonderful
Music by: Jerry Bock
Lyrics by: Sheldon Harnick
Show: Mr. Wonderful
Opening: March 1956

Music of the Night
Music by: Andrew Lloyd Webber
Lyrics by: Charles Hart
Show: Phantom of the Opera
Opening: January 1988

My Best Girl
Music by: Jerry Herman
Lyrics by: Jerry Herman
Show: Mame
Opening: May 1966

My Cup Runneth Over
Music by: Harvey Schmidt
Lyrics by: Tom Jones
Show: I Do! I Do!
Opening: December 1966

My Darling, My Darling
Music by: Frank Loesser
Lyrics by: Frank Loesser
Show: Where's Charley?
Opening: October 1948

My Defenses are Down
Music by: Irving Berlin
Lyrics by: Irving Berlin
Show: Annie Get Your Gun
Opening: May 1946

My Favorite Things
Music by: Richard Rodgers
Lyrics by: Oscar Hammerstein II
Show: Sound of Music
Opening: November 1959

My Funny Valentine
Music by: Richard Rodgers
Lyrics by: Lorenz Hart
Show: Babes in Arms
Opening: April 1937

My Heart Belongs to Daddy
Music by: Cole Porter
Lyrics by: Cole Porter
Show: Leave It to Me
Opening: November 1938

My Heart Stood Still
Music by: Richard Rodgers
Lyrics by: Lorenz Hart
Show: Connecticut Yankee
Opening: November 1927

My Hero
Music by: Oscar Straus
Lyrics by: Stanislaus Stange
Show: Chocolate Soldier
Opening: September 1909

My Man
Music by: Maurice Yvain
Lyrics by: Channing Pollock
Show: Ziegfeld Follies
Opening: June 1921

My Romance
Music by: Richard Rodgers
Lyrics by: Lorenz Hart
Show: Jumbo
Opening: November 1935

My Ship
Music by: Kurt Weill
Lyrics by: Ira Gershwin
Show: Lady in the Dark
Opening: January 1941

My Song
Music by: Ray Henderson
Lyrics by: Lew Brown
Show: George White's Scandals
(11th Edition)
Opening: September 1931

'Neath the Southern Moon
Music by: Victor Herbert
Lyrics by: Rida Johnson Young
Show: Naughty Marietta
Opening: November 1910

Neopolitan Love Song
Music by: Victor Herbert
Lyrics by: Henry Blossom
Show: Princess Pat
Opening: September 1915

Never Never Land
Music by: Jule Styne
Lyrics by: Adolph Green & Betty
Comden
Show: Peter Pan
Opening: October 1954

Never on Sunday
Music by: Manos Hadjidakis
Lyrics by: Joe Darion
Show: Illya Darling
Opening: April 1967

New Sun in the Sky
Music by: Arthur Schwartz
Lyrics by: Howard Dietz
Show: Band Wagon
Opening: June 1931

New York, New York
Music by: Leonard Bernstein
Lyrics by: Adolph Green & Betty Comden
Show: On the Town
Opening: December 1944

Night and Day
Music by: Cole Porter
Lyrics by: Cole Porter
Show: Gay Divorce
Opening: November 1932

Night Was Made for Love, The
Music by: Jerome Kern
Lyrics by: Otto Harbach
Show: Cat and the Fiddle
Opening: October 1931

No, No, Nanette
Music by: Vincent Youmans
Lyrics by: Irving Caesar
Show: No, No, Nanette
Opening: September 1925

No Other Love
Music by: Richard Rodgers
Lyrics by: Oscar Hammerstein II
Show: Me and Juliet
Opening: May 1953

Not for All the Rice in China
Music by: Irving Berlin
Lyrics by: Irving Berlin
Show: As Thousands Cheer
Opening: September 1933

Oh, How I Hate to Get Up in the Morning
Music by: Irving Berlin
Lyrics by: Irving Berlin
Show: Yip, Yip, Yaphank
Opening: September 1918

Oh, What a Beautiful Mornin'
Music by: Richard Rodgers
Lyrics by: Oscar Hammerstein
Show: Oklahoma!
Opening: March 1943

Oh! Gee, Oh! Gosh, Oh! Golly, I'm in Love
Music by: Ole Olsen
Lyrics by: Chic Johnson &
Ernest Brewer
Show: Ziegfeld Follies of 1922
Opening: June 1922

Oh! Lady Be Good

Music by: George Gershwin
Lyrics by: Ira Gershwin
Show: Lady, Be Good!
Opening: December 1924

Ohio

Music by: Leonard Bernstein
Lyrics by: Adolph Green & Betty Comden
Show: Wonderful Town
Opening: February 1953

Oklahoma

Music by: Richard Rodgers
Lyrics by: Oscar Hammerstein II
Show: Oklahoma!
Opening: March 1943

Ol' Man River

Music by: Jerome Kern
Lyrics by: Oscar Hammerstein II
Show: Showboat
Opening: December 1927

Old Devil Moon

Music by: Burton Lane
Lyrics by: E.Y. Harburg
Show: Finian's Rainbow
Opening: January 1947

On a Clear Day

Music by: Burton Lane
Lyrics by: Alan Jay Lerner
Show: On a Clear Day You Can See
        Forever
Opening: October 1965

On the Side of the Angels

Music by: Jerry Bock
Lyrics by: Sheldon Harnick
Show: Fiorello!
Opening: November 1959

On the Street Where You Live

Music by: Frederick Loewe
Lyrics by: Alan Jay Lerner
Show: My Fair Lady
Opening: March 1956

On the Sunny Side of the Street

Music by: Jimmy McHugh
Lyrics by: Dorothy Fields
Show: International Revue
Opening: February 1930

Once in a Lifetime

Music by: Anthony Newley
Lyrics by: Leslie Bricusse
Show: Stop the World -- I Want
        to Get Off
Opening: October 1962

Once in Love with Amy

Music by: Frank Loesser
Lyrics by: Frank Loesser
Show: Where's Charley?
Opening: October 1948

Once Upon a Time

Music by: Charles Strouse
Lyrics by: Lee Adams
Show: All American
Opening: March 1962

One

Music by: Marvin Hamlisch
Lyrics by: Edward Kleban
Show: Chorus Line
Opening: April 1975

One Alone

Music by: Sigmund Romberg
Lyrics by: Otto Harbach & Oscar
        Hammerstein II
Show: Desert Song
Opening: November 1926

One Kiss

Music by: Sigmund Romberg
Lyrics by: Oscar Hammerstein II
Show: New Moon
Opening: September 1928

Only a Rose

Music by: Rudolf Friml
Lyrics by: Brian Hooker &
        W.H. Post
Show: Vagabond King
Opening: September 1925

Out of My Dreams
Music by: Richard Rodgers
Lyrics by: Oscar Hammerstein II
Show: Oklahoma!
Opening: March 1943

Papa, Won't You Dance with Me?
Music by: Jule Styne
Lyrics by: Sammy Cahn
Show: High Button Shoes
Opening: October 1947

Party's Over, The
Music by: Jule Styne
Lyrics by: Adolph Green & Betty
          Comden
Show: Bells are Ringing
Opening: November 1956

People
Music by: Jule Styne
Lyrics by: Bob Merrill
Show: Funny Girl
Opening: March 1964

People Will Say We're in Love
Music by: Richard Rodgers
Lyrics by: Oscar Hammerstein II
Show: Oklahoma!
Opening: March 1943

Play, Gypsies--Dance, Gypsies
Music by: Emmerich Kalman
Lyrics by: Harry Smith
Show: Countess Maritza
Opening: September 1926

Play a Simple Melody
Music by: Irving Berlin
Lyrics by: Irving Berlin
Show: Watch Your Step
Opening: December 1914

Pocketful of Dreams
Music by: Harold Rome
Lyrics by: Harold Rome
Show: Michael Todd's Peep Show
Opening: June 1950

Politics and Poker
Music by: Jerry Bock
Lyrics by: Sheldon Harnick
Show: Fiorello!
Opening: November 1959

Pore Jud
Music by: Richard Rodgers
Lyrics by: Oscar Hammerstein II
Show: Oklahoma!
Opening: March 1943

Pretty Girl is Like a Melody, A
Music by: Irving Berlin
Lyrics by: Irving Berlin
Show: Yip, Yip, Yaphank
Opening: September 1918

Promises, Promises
Music by: Burt Bacharach
Lyrics by: Hal David
Show: Promises, Promises
Opening: December 1968

Put on a Happy Face
Music by: Charles Strouse
Lyrics by: Lee Adams
Show: Bye Bye Birdie
Opening: April 1960

Put Your Arms Around Me Honey
Music by: Albert Von Tilzer
Lyrics by: Junie McCree
Show: Madame Sherry
Opening: August 1910

Quiet Night
Music by: Richard Rodgers
Lyrics by: Lorenz Hart
Show: On Your Toes
Opening: April 1936

Rain in Spain
Music by: Frederick Loewe
Lyrics by: Alan Jay Lerner
Show: My Fair Lady
Opening: March 1956

Real Live Girl
Music by: Cy Coleman
Lyrics by: Carolyn Leigh
Show: Little Me
Opening: November 1962

Real Nice Clambake, A
Music by: Richard Rodgers
Lyrics by: Oscar Hammerstein II
Show: Carousel
Opening: April 1945

Rhapsody in Blue
Music by: George Gershwin
Lyrics by: Instrumental
Show: George White's Scandals
        (8th Edition)
Opening: June 1926

Rhode Island is Famous for You
Music by: Arthur Schwartz
Lyrics by: Howard Dietz
Show: Inside U.S.A.
Opening: April 1948

Ribbons Down My Back
Music by: Jerry Herman
Lyrics by: Jerry Herman
Show: Hello, Dolly!
Opening: January 1964

Ridin' High
Music by: Cole Porter
Lyrics by: Cole Porter
Show: Red, Hot and Blue!
Opening: October 1936

Riff Song
Music by: Sigmund Romberg
Lyrics by: Otto Harbach & Oscar
        Hammerstein II
Show: Desert Song
Opening: November 1926

Right as the Rain
Music by: Harold Arlen
Lyrics by: E.Y. Harburg
Show: Bloomer Girl
Opening: October 1944

Rio Rita
Music by: Harry Tierney
Lyrics by: Joseph McCarthy
Show: Rio Rita
Opening: Febrary 1927

Rock Island
Music by: Meredith Willson
Lyrics by: Meredith Willson
Show: Music Man
Opening: December 1957

Rock-a-Bye Your Baby With a Dixie Melody
Music by: Jean Schwartz
Lyrics by: Sam Lewis & Joe Young
Show: Sinbad
Opening: February 1918

Romance
Music by: Sigmund Romberg
Lyrics by: Otto Harbach & Oscar
        Hammerstein II
Show: Desert Song
Opening: November 1926

Room Without Windows, A
Music by: Ervin Drake
Lyrics by: Ervin Drake
Show: What Makes Sammy Run?
Opening: February 1964

Rose-Marie
Music by: Rudolf Friml
Lyrics by: Otto Harbach & Oscar
        Hammerstein II
Show: Rose-Marie
Opening: September 1924

'S Wonderful
Music by: George Gershwin
Lyrics by: Ira Gershwin
Show: Funny Face
Opening: November 1927

Saga of Jenny
Music by: Kurt Weill
Lyrics by: Ira Gershwin
Show: Lady in the Dark
Opening: January 1941

Saturday Night in Cental Park
Music by: Richard Lewine
Lyrics by: Arnold Horwitt
Show: Make Mine Manhattan
Opening: January 1948

Say, Darling
Music by: Jule Styne
Lyrics by: Adolph Green & Betty
            Comden
Show: Say, Darling
Opening: April 1958

Say It with Music
Music by: Irving Berlin
Lyrics by: Irving Berlin
Show: Music Box Revue
Opening: October 1922

Second Hand Rose
Music by: James Hanley
Lyrics by: Grant Clarke
Show: Ziegfeld Follies
Opening: June 1921

Send in the Clowns
Music by: Stephen Sondheim
Lyrics by: Hugh Wheeler
Show: A Little Night Music
Opening: February 1973

Sentimental Me
Music by: Richard Rodgers
Lyrics by: Lorenz Hart
Show: Garrick Gaieties
Opening: May 1925

September Song
Music by: Kurt Weill
Lyrics by: Maxwell Anderson
Show: Knickerbocker Holiday
Opening: October 1938

Seventy-Six Trombones
Music by: Meredith Willson
Lyrics by: Meredith Willson
Show: Music Man
Opening: December 1957

Shall We Dance?
Music by: Richard Rodgers
Lyrics by: Oscar Hammerstein
Show: King and I
Opening: March 1951

Shalom
Music by: Jerry Herman
Lyrics by: Jerry Herman
Show: Milk and Honey
Opening: October 1961

She Didn't Say "Yes"
Music by: Jerome Kern
Lyrics by: Otto Harbach
Show: Cat and the Fiddle
Opening: October 1931

She Loves Me
Music by: Jerry Bock
Lyrics by: Sheldon Harnick
Show: She Loves Me
Opening: Aapril 1963

Shine on Your Shoes, A
Music by: Arthur Schwartz
Lyrics by: Howard Dietz
Show: Flying Colors
Opening: September 1932

Sing for Your Supper
Music by: Richard Rodgers
Lyrics by: Lorenz Hart
Show: Boys from Syacuse
Opening: November 1938

Sit Down You're Rockin' the Boat
Music by: Frank Loesser
Lyrics by: Frank Loesser
Show: Guys and Dolls
Opening: November 1950

Sixteen Going on Seventeen
Music by: Richard Rodgers
Lyrics by: Oscar Hammerstein II
Show: Sound of Music
Opening: November 1959

Slaughter on Tenth Avenue
Music by: Richard Rodgers
Lyrics by: Instrumental
Show: On Your Toes
Opening: April 1936

Small World
Music by: Jule Styne
Lyrics by: Stephen Sondheim
Show: Gypsy
Opening: May 1959

Smoke Gets in our Eyes
Music by: Jerome Kern
Lyrics by: Otto Harbach
Show: Roberta
Opening: November 1933

So Far
Music by: Richard Rodgers
Lyrics by: Oscar Hammerstein II
Show: Allegro
Opening: October 1947

So in Love
Music by: Cole Porter
Lyrics by: Cole Porter
Show: Kiss Me Kate
Opening: December 1940

So Long, Farewell
Music by: Richard Rodgers
Lyrics by: Oscar Hammerstein II
Show: Sound of Music
Opening: November 1959

Soft Lights and Sweet Music
Music by: Irving Berlin
Lyrics by: Irving Berlin
Show: Face the Music
Opening: February 1932

Softly, As in a Morning Sunrise
Music by: Sigmund Romberg
Lyrics by: Oscar Hammerstein II
Show: New Moon
Opening: September 1928

Soliloquy (Carousel)
Music by: Richard Rodgers
Lyrics by: Oscar Hammerstein
Show: Carousel
Opening: April 1945

Some Enchanted Evening
Music by: Richard Rodgers
Lyrics by: Oscar Hammerstein II
Show: South Pacific
Opening: April 1949

Some Day
Music by: Rudolf Friml
Lyrics by: Brian Hooker &
              W.H. Post
Show: Vagabond King
Opening: September 1925

Some Other Time
Music by: Leonard Bernstein
Lyrics by: Adolph Green & Betty
              Comden
Show: On the Town
Opening: December 1944

Somebody Loves Me
Music by: George Gershwin
Lyrics by: B.G. DaSylva & Ballard
              Macdonald
Show: George White's Scandals
        (6th Edition)
Opening: June 1924

Someone to Watch Over Me
Music by: George Gershwin
Lyrics by: Ira Gershwin
Show: Oh, Kay!
Opening: November 1926

Something for the Boys
Music by: Cole Porter
Lyrics by: Cole Porter
Show: Something for the Boys
Opening: January 1943

Something to Remember You By
Music by: Arthur Schwartz
Lyrics by: Howard Dietz
Show: Three's a Crowd
Opening: October 1930

Something Wonderful
Music by: Richard Rodgers
Lyrics by: Oscar Hammerstein II
Show: King and I
Opening: March 1951

Something's Always Happening on the River
Music by: Jule Styne
Lyrics by: Adolph Green & Betty Comden
Show: Say, Darling
Opening: April 1958

Something's Coming
Music by: Leonard Bernstein
Lyrics by: Stephen Sondheim
Show: West Side Story
Opening: September 1957

Sometimes I'm Happy
Music by: Vincent Youmans
Lyrics by: Clifford Grey & Leo Robbins
Show: Hit the Deck
Opening: April 1927

Somewhere
Music by: Leonard Bernstein
Lyrics by: Stephen Sondheim
Show: West Side Story
Opening: September 1957

Song is You, The
Music by: Jerome Kern
Lyrics by: Oscar Hammerstein II
Show: Music in the Air
Opening: November 1932

Song of the Vagabonds
Music by: Rudolf Friml
Lyrics by: Brian Hooker & W.H. Post
Show: Vagabond King
Opening: September 1925

Soon
Music by: George Gershwin
Lyrics by: Ira Gershwin
Show: Strike Up the Band
Opening: January 1930

Soon It's Gonna Rain
Music by: Harvey Schmidt
Lyrics by: Tom Jones
Show: Fantasticks
Opening: May 1960

Sound of Music, The
Music by: Richard Rodgers
Lyrics by: Oscar Hammerstein II
Show: Sound of Music
Opening: November 1959

South America, Take It Away
Music by: Harold Rome
Lyrics by: Harold Rome
Show: Call Me Mister
Opening: April 1946

Speak Low
Music by: Kurt Weill
Lyrics by: Ogden Nash
Show: One Touch of Venus
Opening: October 1943

Spring is Here
Music by: Richard Rodgers
Lyrics by: Lorenz Hart
Show: I Married an Angel
Opening: May 1938

Strike Up the Band
Music by: George Gershwin
Lyrics by: Ira Gershwin
Show: Strike Up the Band
Opening: January 1930

Standing on the Corner
Music by: Frank Loesser
Lyrics by: Frank Loesser
Show: Most Happy Fella
Opening: May 1956

Steam Heat
Music by: Richard Adler
Lyrics by: Jerry Ross
Show: Pajama Game
Opening: May 1954

Stouthearted Men
Music by: Sigmund Romberg
Lyrics by: Oscar Hammerstein II
Show: New Moon
Opening: September 1928

Strange Music
Music by: Edvard Grieg
Lyrics by: Robert Wright & George Forrest
Show: Song of Norway
Opening: August 1944

Stranger in Paradise
Music by: Alexander Borodin
Lyrics by: Robert Wright & George Forrest
Show: Kismet
Opening: December 1953

Strike Me Pink
Music by: Ray Henderson
Lyrics by: Lew Brown
Show: Strike Me Pink
Opening: March 1933

Summertime
Music by: George Gershwin
Lyrics by: DuBose Heyward
Show: Porgy and Bess
Opening: October 1935

Summertime Love
Music by: Frank Loesser
Lyrics by: Frank Loesser
Show: Greenwillow
Opening: March 1960

Sunny
Music by: Jerome Kern
Lyrics by: Otto Harbach & Oscar
            Hammerstein II
Show: Sunny
Opening: September 1925

Sunrise, Sunset
Music by: Jerry Bock
Lyrics by: Sheldon Harnick
Show: Fiddler on the Roof
Opening: September 1964

Superstar
Music by: Andrew Lloyd Webber
Lyrics by: Tim Rice
Show: Jesus Christ Superstar
Opening: October 1971

**Surrey With the Fringe on
Top, The**
Music by: Richard Rodgers
Lyrics by: Oscar Hammerstein II
Show: Oklahoma!
Opening: March 1943

Sweetest Sounds
Music by: Richard Rodgers
Lyrics by: Richard Rodgers
Show: No Strings
Opening: March 1962

Sweethearts
Music by: Victor Herbert
Lyrics by: Robert B.Smith
Show: Sweethearts
Opening: September 1913

Sympathy
Music by: Rudolf Friml
Lyrics by: Otto Harbach
Show: Firefly
Opening: December 1912

Sympathy
Music by: Oscar Straus
Lyrics by: Stanislaus Stange
Show: Chocolate Soldier
Opening: September 1909

Take Me Along
Music by: Bob Merrill
Lyrics by: Bob Merrill
Show: Take Me Along
Opening: October 1959

Taking a Chance on Love
Music by: Vernon Duke
Lyrics by: Ted Fetter
Show: Cabin in the Sky
Opening: October 1940

Tea for Two
Music by: Vincent Youmans
Lyrics by: Irving Caesar
Show: No, No, Nanette
Opening: September 1925

Tell Me Pretty Maiden
Music by: Leslie Stuart
Lyrics by: Leslie Stuart
Show: Florodora
Opening: November 1900

Ten Cents a Dance
Music by: Richard Rodgers
Lyrics by: Lorenz Hart
Show: Simple Simon
Opening: February 1930

Thank Your Father
Music by: Ray Henderson
Lyrics by: B.G. DeSylva and
            Lew Brown
Show: Flying High
Opening: March 1930

That Great Come-and-Get-It Day
Music by: Burton Lane
Lyrics by: E.Y. Harburg
Show: Finian's Rainbow
Opening: January 1947

That's All
Music by: Cole Porter
Lyrics by: Cole Porter
Show: Silk Stockings
Opening: February 1955

That's Why Darkies Were Born
Music by: Ray Henderson
Lyrics by: Lew Brown
Show: George White's Scandals
        (11th Edition)
Opening: September 1931

There But for You Go I
Music by: Frederick Loewe
Lyrics by: Alan Jay Lerner
Show: Brigadoon
Opening: March 1947

There is Nothin ' Like a Dame
Music by: Richard Rodgers
Lyrics by: Oscar Hammerstein II
Show: South Pacific
Opening: April 1949

There's a Great Day Coming Manana
Music by: Burton Lane
Lyrics by: E.Y. Harburg
Show: Hold On to Your Hats
Opening: September 1940

There's a Boat dat's Leavin' Soon for New York
Music by: George Gershwin
Lyrics by: Ira Gershwin
Show: Porgy and Bess
Opening: October 1935

There's a Small Hotel
Music by: Richard Rodgers
Lyrics by: Lorenz Hart
Show: On Your Toes
Opening: April 1936

There's No Business Like Show Business
Music by: Irving Berlin
Lyrics by: Irving Berlin
Show: Annie Get Your Gun
Opening: May 1946

They Call the Wind Maria
Music by: Frederick Loewe
Lyrics by: Alan Jay Lerner
Show: Paint Your Wagon
Opening: November 1951

They Didn't Believe Me
Music by: Jerome Kern
Lyrics by: Herbert Reynolds
Show: Girl from Utah
Opening: August 1914

They Say It's Wonderful
Music by: Irving Berlin
Lyrics by: Irving Berlin
Show: Annie Get Your Gun
Opening: May 1946

This Can't Be Love
Music by: Richard Rodgers
Lyrics by: Lorenz Hart
Show: Boys from Syacuse
Opening: November 1938

This is the Army, Mr. Jones
Music by: Irving Berlin
Lyrics by: Irving Berlin
Show: This is the Army
Opening: July 1942

This is the Missus
Music by: Ray Henderson
Lyrics by: Lew Brown
Show: George White's Scandals
(11th Edition)
Opening: September 1931

This Nearly Was Mine
Music by: Richard Rodgers
Lyrics by: Oscar Hammerstein II
Show: South Pacific
Opening: April 1949

Thou Swell
Music by: Richard Rodgers
Lyrics by: Lorenz Hart
Show: Connecticut Yankee
Opening: November 1927

Thrill is Gone, The
Music by: Ray Henderson
Lyrics by: Lew Brown
Show: George White's Scandals
(11th Edition)
Opening: September 1931

Through the Years
Music by: Vincent Youmans
Lyrics by: Edward Heyman
Show: Through the Years
Opening: January 1932

'Til Tomorrow
Music by: Jerry Bock
Lyrics by: Sheldon Harnick
Show: Fiorello!
Opening: November 1959

Till the Clouds Roll By
Music by: Jerome Kern
Lyrics by: P.G. Wodehouse
Show: Oh, Boy!
Opening: February 1917

Till There Was You
Music by: Meredith Willson
Lyrics by: Meredith Willson
Show: Music Man
Opening: December 1957

Time on My Hands
Music by: Vincent Youmans
Lyrics by: Harold Adamson &
Mack Gordon
Show: Smiles
Opening: November 1930

To Life (L'Chaim)
Music by: Jerry Bock
Lyrics by: Sheldon Harnick
Show: Fiddler on the Roof
Opening: September 1964

Together
Music by: Jule Styne
Lyrics by: Stephen Sondheim
Show: Gypsy
Opening: May 1959

Tomorrow
Music by: Charles Strouse
Lyrics by: Martin Charnin
Show: Annie
Opening: April 1977

Tonight
Music by: Leonard Bernstein
Lyrics by: Stephen Sondheim
Show: West Side Story
Opening: September 1957

Too Close for Comfort
Music by: Jerry Bock
Lyrics by: Sheldon Harnick
Show: Mr. Wonderful
Opening: March 1956

Too Darn Hot
Music by: Cole Porter
Lyrics by: Cole Porter
Show: Kiss Me Kate
Opening: December 1940

Totem Tom-Tom
Music by: Rudolf Friml
Lyrics by: Otto Harbach & Oscar
            Hammerstein II
Show: Rose-Marie
Opening: September 1924

Touch of Your Hand, The
Music by: Jerome Kern
Lyrics by: Otto Harbach
Show: Roberta
Opening: November 1933

Toyland
Music by: Victor Herbert
Lyrics by: Glen MacDonough
Show: Babes in Toyland
Opening: October 1903

Tradition
Music by: Jerry Bock
Lyrics by: Sheldon Harnick
Show: Fiddler on the Roof
Opening: September 1964

Tramp! Tramp! Tramp!
Music by: Victor Herbert
Lyrics by: Rida Johnson Young
Show: Naughty Marietta
Opening: November 1910

Treat Me Rough
Music by: George Gershwin
Lyrics by: Ira Gershwin
Show: Girl Crazy
Opening: October 1930

Try to Remember
Music by: Harvey Schmidt
Lyrics by: Tom Jones
Show: Fantasticks
Opening: May 1960

Use Your Imagination
Music by: Cole Porter
Lyrics by: Cole Porter
Show: Out of This World
Opening: December 1950

Varsity Drag
Music by: Ray Henderson
Lyrics by: B.G. DeSylva and
            Lew Brown
Show: Good News!
Opening: September 1927

Wait Till You See Her
Music by: Richard Rodgers
Lyrics by: Lorenz Hart
Show: By Jupiter
Opening: November 1938

Wanting You
Music by: Sigmund Romberg
Lyrics by: Oscar Hammerstein II
Show: New Moon
Opening: September 1928

We Kiss in a Shadow
Music by: Richard Rodgers
Lyrics by: Oscar Hammerstein II
Show: King and I
Opening: March 1951

We Need a Little Christmas
Music by: Jerry Herman
Lyrics by: Jerry Herman
Show: Mame
Opening: May 1966

We Open in Venice
Music by: Cole Porter
Lyrics by: Cole Porter
Show: Kiss Me Kate
Opening: December 1940

Well, Did You Evah?
Music by: Cole Porter
Lyrics by: Cole Porter
Show: DuBarry Was a Lady
Opening: December 1939

Wells Fargo Wagon
Music by: Meredith Willson
Lyrics by: Meredith Willson
Show: Music Man
Opening: December 1957

Were Thine That Special Face
Music by: Cole Porter
Lyrics by: Cole Porter
Show: Kiss Me Kate
Opening: December 1940

What Did I Have That I Don't Have?
Music by: Burton Lane
Lyrics by: Alan Jay Lerner
Show: On a Clear Day You Can
See Forever
Opening: October 1965

What Do the Simple Folk Do?
Music by: Frederick Loewe
Lyrics by: Alan Jay Lerner
Show: Camelot
Opening: December 1960

What Do You Think I Am?
Music by: Hugh Martin
Lyrics by: Ralph Blane
Show: Best Foot Forward
Opening: October 1941

What I Did for Love
Music by: Marvin Hamlisch
Lyrics by: Edward Kleban
Show: Chorus Line
Opening: April 1975

What is There to Say?
Music by: Vernon Duke
Lyrics by: E.Y. Harburg
Show: Ziegfeld Follies
Opening: January 1934

What is This Thing Called Love?
Music by: Cole Porter
Lyrics by: Cole Porter
Show: Wake Up and Dream
Opening: December 1929

What Kind of Fool Am I?
Music by: Anthony Newley
Lyrics by: Leslie Bricusse
Show: Stop the World --
I Want to Get Off
Opening: October 1962

What's the Use of Wond'rin'
Music by: Richard Rodgers
Lyrics by: Oscar Hammerstein II
Show: Carousel
Opening: April 1945

Whatever Lola Wants
Music by: Richard Adler
Lyrics by: Jerry Ross
Show: Damn Yankees
Opening: May 1955

When I'm Not Near the Girl I Love
Music by: Burton Lane
Lyrics by: E.Y. Harburg
Show: Finian's Rainbow
Opening: January 1947

When the Boys Come Home
Music by: Harold Arlen
Lyrics by: E.Y. Harburg
Show: Bloomer Girl
Opening: October 1944

Where is Love?
Music by: Lionel Bart
Lyrics by: Lionel Bart
Show: Oliver!
Opening: January 1963

Where is the Life That Late I Led?
Music by: Cole Porter
Lyrics by: Cole Porter
Show: Kiss Me Kate
Opening: December 1940

Where or When
Music by: Richard Rodgers
Lyrics by: Lorenz Hart
Show: Babes in Arms
Opening: April 1937

Who Can I Turn To?
Music by: Anthony Newley
Lyrics by: Leslie Bricusse
Show: Roar of the Greasepaint--
       The Smell of the Crowd
Opening: May 1965

Who Cares?
Music by: George Gershwin
Lyrics by: Ira Gershwin
Show: Of Thee I Sing
Opening: December 1931

Who?
Music by: Jerome Kern
Lyrics by: Otto Harbach & Oscar
           Hammerstein II
Show: Sunny
Opening: September 1925

Why Shouldn't I?
Music by: Cole Porter
Lyrics by: Cole Porter
Show: Jubilee
Opening: October 1935

Why Can't You Behave?
Music by: Cole Porter
Lyrics by: Cole Porter
Show: Kiss Me Kate
Opening: December 1940

Why Do I Love You?
Music by: Jerome Kern
Lyrics by: Oscar Hammerstein II
Show: Showboat
Opening: December 1927

Why Shouldn't I?
Music by: Cole Porter
Lyrics by: Cole Porter
Show: Jubilee
Opening: October 1935

Why Was I Born?
Music by: Jerome Kern
Lyrics by: Oscar Hammerstein II
Show: Sweet Adeline
Opening: September 1929

Will You Remember?
Music by: Sigmund Romberg
Lyrics by: Rida Johnson Young
Show: Maytime
Opening: August 1917

Wintergreen for President
Music by: George Gershwin
Lyrics by: Ira Gershwin
Show: Of Thee I Sing
Opening: December 1931

Wish You Were Here
Music by: Harold Rome
Lyrics by: Harold Rome
Show: Wish You Were Here
Opening: June 1952

With a Little Bit of Luck
Music by: Frederick Loewe
Lyrics by: Alan Jay Lerner
Show: My Fair Lady
Opening: March 1956

With a Song in My Hert
Music by: Richard Rodgers
Lyrics by: Lorenz Hart
Show: Spring is Here
Opening: March 1929

Without a Song
Music by: Vincent Youmans
Lyrics by: Billy Rose and Edward
           Eliscu
Show: Great Day!
Opening: October 1929

Wonderful Day Like Today, A
Music by: Anthony Newley
Lyrics by: Leslie Bricusse
Show: Roar of the Greasepaint
       -- The Smell of the Crowd
Opening: May 1965

Wonderful Guy, A
Music by: Richard Rodgers
Lyrics by: Oscar Hammerstein
Show: South Pacific
Opening: April 1949

World in My Arms, The
Music by: Burton Lane
Lyrics by: E.Y. Harburg
Show: Hold On to Your Hats
Opening: September 1940

Wouldn't It Be Loverly?
Music by: Frederick Loewe
Lyrics by: Alan Jay Lerner
Show: My Fair Lady
Opening: March 1956

Wunderbar
Music by: Cole Porter
Lyrics by: Cole Porter
Show: Kiss Me Kate
Opening: December 1940

Yankee Doodle Boy
Music by: George M. Cohan
Lyrics by: George M. Cohan
Show: Little Johnny Jones
Opening: November 1904

Yesterdays
Music by: Jerome Kern
Lyrics by: Otto Harbach
Show: Roberta
Opening: November 1933

You and the Night and the Music
Music by: Arthur Schwartz
Lyrics by: Howard Dietz
Show: Revenge with Music
Opening: November 1934

You Are Beautiful
Music by: Richard Rodgers
Lyrics by: Oscar Hammerstein II
Show: Flower Drum Song
Opening: December 1958

You Are Love
Music by: Jerome Kern
Lyrics by: Oscar Hammerstein II
Show: Showboat
Opening: December 1927

You Are Never Away
Music by: Richard Rodgers
Lyrics by: Oscar Hammerstein II
Show: Allegro
Opening: October 1947

You Are Woman
Music by: Jule Styne
Lyrics by: Bob Merrill
Show: Funny Girl
Opening: March 1964

You Can't Get a Man with a Gun
Music by: Irving Berlin
Lyrics by: Irving Berlin
Show: Annie Get Your Gun
Opening: May 1946

You Do Something to Me
Music by: Cole Porter
Lyrics by: Cole Porter
Show: Fifty Million Frenchmen
Opening: November 1929

You Took Advantage of Me
Music by: Richard Rodgers
Lyrics by: Lorenz Hart
Show: Present Arms
Opening: April 1928

You Were Meant for Me
Music by: Eubie Blake
Lyrics by: Noble Sissle
Show: Andre Charlot's Revue
of 1924
Opening: January 1924

You'll Never Get Away from Me
Music by: Jule Styne
Lyrics by: Stephen Sondheim
Show: Gypsy
Opening: May 1959

You'll Never Walk Alone
Music by: Richard Rodgers
Lyrics by: Oscar Hammerstein II
Show: Carousel
Opening: April 1945

You're a Builder-Upper
Music by: Harold Arlen
Lyrics by: E.Y. Harburg &
            Ira Gershwin
Show: Life Begins at 8:40
Opening: August 1934

You're a Grand Old Flag
Music by: George M. Cohan
Lyrics by: George M. Cohan
Show: George Washington Jr.
Opening: February 1906

You're an Old Smoothie
Music by: Richard A. Whiting
Lyrics by: B.G. DeSylva
Show: Take a Chance
Opening: Novermber 1932

You're Devastating
Music by: Jerome Kern
Lyrics by: Otto Harbach
Show: Roberta
Opening: November 1933

You're Just in Love
Music by: Irving Berlin
Lyrics by: Irving Berlin
Show: Call Me Madam
Opening: October 1950

You're Lonely and I'm Lonely
Music by: Irving Berlin
Lyrics by: Irving Berlin
Show: Louisiana Purchase
Opening: May 1940

You're the Cream in My Coffee
Music by: Ray Henderson
Lyrics by: B.G. DeSylva and Lew
            Brown
Show: Hold Everything
Opening: October 1928

You're the Top
Music by: Cole Porter
Lyrics by: Cole Porter
Show: Anything Goes
Opening: November 1934

You've Got to Be Carefully Taught
Music by: Richard Rodgers
Lyrics by: Oscar Hammerstein II
Show: South Pacific
Opening: April 1949

Young and Foolish
Music by: Albert Hague
Lyrics by: Arnold Horwitt
Show: Plain and Fancy
Opening: January 1955

Younger Than Springtime
Music by: Richard Rodgers
Lyrics by: Oscar Hammerstein II
Show: South Pacific
Opening: April 1949

Your Land and My Land
Music by: Sigmund Romberg
Lyrics by: Dorothy Donnelly
Show: My Maryland
Opening: September 1927

Ziguener
Music by: Noël Coward
Lyrics by: Noël Coward
Show: Bitter Sweet
Opening: November 1929

Section Two

Composers
(Alphabetically Listed)

BROADWAY'S LEADING COMPOSERS

← FREDERICK LOEWE (left) and ALAN JAY LERNER, composer and lyricist for four smash hits on Broadway.

COLE PORTER, Broadway 's (and Hollywood's) composer and lyricist of sparkling sophistication. →

JEROME KERN (right) with OSCAR HAMMERSTEIN II, his major lyricist throughout the 1920's and 1930's.
↓

Richard Adler *(1921-)*

Heart
Show: Damn Yankees
Opened: May 1955
Lyrics by: Jerry Ross

Hernando's Hideaway
Show: Pajama Game
Opened: May 1954
Lyrics by: Jerry Ross

Hey, There
Show: Pajama Game
Opened: May 1954
Lyrics by: Jerry Ross

Steam Heat
Show: Pajama Game
Opened: May 1954
Lyrics by: Jerry Ross

Whatever Lola Wants
Show: Damn Yankees
Opened: May 1955
Lyrics by: Jerry Ross

Harold Arlen *(1905-1986)*

Come Rain or Come Shine
Show: St. Louis Woman
Opened: March 1946
Lyrics by: Johnny Mercer

Eagle and Me, The
Show: Bloomer Girl
Opened: October 1944
Lyrics by: E.Y. Harburg

Learn to Croon
Show: You Said It
Opened: January 1931
Lyrics by: Jack Yellen

Let's Take a Walk Around the Block
Show: Life Begins at 8:40
Opened: August 1934
Lyrics by: E.Y. Harburg & Ira
  Gershwin

Harold Arlen (continued)

Right as the Rain
Show: Bloomer Girl
Opened: October 1944
Lyrics by: E.Y. Harburg

When the Boys Come Home
Show: Bloomer Girl
Opened: October 1944
Lyrics by: E.Y. Harburg

You're a Builder-Upper
Show: Life Begins at 8:40
Opened: August 1934
Lyrics by: E.Y. Harburg & Ira
  Gershwin

Burt Bacharach *(1929-)*

I'll Never Fall in Love Again
Show: Promises, Promises
Opened: December 1968
Lyrics by: Hal David

Promises, Promises
Show: Promises, Promises
Opened: December 1968
Lyrics by: Hal David

Lionel Bart *(1930-)*

As Long As He Needs Me
Show: Oliver!
Opened: January 1963
Lyrics by: Lionel Bart

I'd Do Anything
Show: Oliver!
Opened: January 1963
Lyrics by: Lionel Bart

Where is Love?
Show: Oliver!
Opened: January 1963
Lyrics by: Lionel Bart

Irving Berlin *(1888-1990)*

American Eagles
Show: This is the Army
Opened: July 1942
Lyrics by: Irving Berlin

Irving Berlin (continued)

Anything You Can Do
Show: Annie Get Your Gun
Opened: May 1946
Lyrics by: Irving Berlin

Best Thing for You, The
Show: Call Me Madam
Opened: October 1950
Lyrics by: Irving Berlin

Blue Skies
Show: Betsy
Opened: December 1926
Lyrics by: Irving Berlin

Doin' What Comes Natur'lly
Show: Annie Get Your Gun
Opened: May 1946
Lyrics by: Irving Berlin

Easter Parade
Show: As Thousands Cheer
Opened: September 1933
Lyrics by: Irving Berlin

Fools Fall in Love
Show: Louisiana Purchase
Opened: May 1940
Lyrics by: Irving Berlin

The Girl That I Marry
Show: Annie Get Your Gun
Opened: May 1946
Lyrics by: Irving Berlin

Heat Wave
Show: As Thousands Cheer
Opened: September 1933
Lyrics by: Irving Berlin

The Hostess with the Mostes' on the Ball
Show: Call Me Madam
Opened: October 1950
Lyrics by: Irving Berlin

Irving Berlin (continued)

I Got Lost in His Arms
Show: Annie Get Your Gun
Opened: May 1946
Lyrics by: Irving Berlin

I Got the Sun in the Morning
Show: Annie Get Your Gun
Opened: May 1946
Lyrics by: Irving Berlin

I Left My Heart at the Stage Door Canteen
Show: This is the Army
Opened: July 1942
Lyrics by: Irving Berlin

I Love a Piano
Show: Stop! Look! Listen!
Opened: December 1915
Lyrics by: Irving Berlin

I'm An Indian, Too
Show: Annie Get Your Gun
Opened: May 1946
Lyrics by: Irving Berlin

It's a Lovely Day Today
Show: Call Me Madam
Opened: October 1950
Lyrics by: Irving Berlin

It's a Lovely Day Tomorrow
Show: Louisiana Purchase
Opened: May 1940
Lyrics by: Irving Berlin

Lady of the Evening
Show: Music Box Revue
Opened: October 1922
Lyrics by: Irving Berlin

Let's Have Another Cup o' Coffee
Show: Face the Music
Opened: February 1932
Lyrics by: Irving Berlin

<u>Irving Berlin</u> (continued)

Let's Take an Old Fashioned Walk
Show: Miss Liberty
Opened: July 1949
Lyrics by: Irving Berlin

Mandy
Show: Yip, Yip, Yaphank
Opened: September 1918
Lyrics by: Irving Berlin

My Defenses are Down
Show: Annie Get Your Gun
Opened: May 1946
Lyrics by: Irving Berlin

Not for All the Rice in China
Show: As Thousands Cheer
Opened: September 1933
Lyrics by: Irving Berlin

Oh, How I Hate to Get Up in the Morning
Show: Yip, Yip, Yaphank
Opened: September 1918
Lyrics by: Irving Berlin

Play a Simple Melody
Show: Watch Your Step
Opened: December 1914
Lyrics by: Irving Berlin

Pretty Girl is Like a Melody, A
Show: Yip, Yip, Yaphank
Opened: September 1918
Lyrics by: Irving Berlin

Say It with Music
Show: Music Box Revue
Opened: October 1922
Lyrics by: Irving Berlin

Soft Lights and Sweet Music
Show: Face theMusic
Opened: February 1932
Lyrics by: Irving Berlin

<u>Irving Berlin</u> (continued)

There's No Business Like Show Business
Show: Annie Get Your Gun
Opened: May 1946
Lyrics by: Irving Berlin

They Say It's Wonderful
Show: Annie Get Your Gun
Opened: May 1946
Lyrics by: Irving Berlin

This is the Army, Mr. Jones
Show: This is the Army
Opened: July 1942
Lyrics by: Irving Berlin

You Can't Get a Man with a Gun
Show: Annie Get Your Gun
Opened: May 1946
Lyrics by: Irving Berlin

You're Just in Love
Show: Call Me Madam
Opened: October 1950
Lyrics by: Irving Berlin

You're Lonely and I'm Lonely
Show: Louisiana Purchase
Opened: May 1940
Lyrics by: Irving Berlin

<u>Leonard Bernstein</u> *(1918-1990)*

America
Show: West Side Story
Opened: September 1957
Lyrics by: Stephen Sondheim

Cool
Show: West Side Story
Opened: September 1957
Lyrics by: Stephen Sondheim

Gee, Officer Krupke
Show: West Side Story
Opened: September 1957
Lyrics by: Stephen Sondheim

Leonard Bernstein (continued)
I Feel Pretty
Show: West Side Story
Opened: September 1957
Lyrics by: Stephen Sondheim

Lonely Town
Show: On the Town
Opened: December 1944
Lyrics by: Adolph Green & Betty Comden

Make Our Garden Grow
Show: Candide
Opened: December 1956
Lyrics by: Richard Wilbur

Maria
Show: West Side Story
Opened: September 1957
Lyrics by: Stephen Sondheim

New York, New York
Show: On the Town
Opened: December 1944
Lyrics by: Adolph Green & Betty Comden

Ohio
Show: Wonderful Town
Opened: February 1953
Lyrics by: Adolph Green & Betty Comden

Some Other Time
Show: On the Town
Opened: December 1944
Lyrics by: Adolph Green & Betty Comden

Something's Coming
Show: West Side Story
Opened: September 1957
Lyrics by: Stephen Sondheim

Somewhere
Show: West Side Story
Opened: September 1957
Lyrics by: Stephen Sondheim

Leonard Bernstein (continued)
Tonight
Show: West Side Story
Opened: September 1957
Lyrics by: Stephen Sondheim

Eubie Blake *(1883-1983)*
I'm Just Wild About Harry
Show: Shuffle Along
Opened: May 1921
Lyrics by: Noble Sissle

You Were Meant for Me
Show: Andre Charlot's Revue of 1924
Opened: January 1924
Lyrics by: Noble Sissle

Jerry Bock *(1928-)*
I Love a Cop
Show: Fiorello!
Opened: November 1959
Lyrics by: Sheldon Harnick

If I Were a Rich Man
Show: Fiddler on the Roof
Opened: September 1964
Lyrics by: Sheldon Harnick

Little Tin Box
Show: Fiorello!
Opened: November 1959
Lyrics by: Sheldon Harnick

Matchmaker, Matchmaker
Show: Fiddler on the Roof
Opened: September 1964
Lyrics by: Sheldon Harnick

Miracle of Miracles
Show: Fiddler on the Roof
Opened: September 1964
Lyrics by: Sheldon Harnick

Mr. Wonderful
Show: Mr. Wonderful
Opened: March 1956
Lyrics by: Sheldon Harnick

Jerry Bock (continued)

On the Side of the Angels
Show: Fiorello!
Opened: November 1959
Lyrics by: Sheldon Harnick

Politics and Poker
Show: Fiorello!
Opened: November 1959
Lyrics by: Sheldon Harnick

She Loves Me
Show: She Loves Me
Opened: Aapril 1963
Lyrics by: Sheldon Harnick

Sunrise, Sunset
Show: Fiddler on the Roof
Opened: September 1964
Lyrics by: Sheldon Harnick

'Til Tomorrow
Show: Fiorello!
Opened: November 1959
Lyrics by: Sheldon Harnick

To Life (L'Chaim)
Show: Fiddler on the Roof
Opened: September 1964
Lyrics by: Sheldon Harnick

Too Close for Comfort
Show: Mr. Wonderful
Opened: March 1956
Lyrics by: Sheldon Harnick

Tradition
Show: Fiddler on the Roof
Opened: September 1964
Lyrics by: Sheldon Harnick

Alexander Borodin *(1833-1887)*

And This is My Beloved
Show: Kismet
Opened: December 1953
Lyrics by: Robert Wright &
George Forrest

Alexander Borodin (continued)

Baubles, Bangles and Beads
Show: Kismet
Opened: December 1953
Lyrics by: Robert Wright &
George Forrest

Stranger in Paradise
Show: Kismet
Opened: December 1953
Lyrics by: Robert Wright &
George Forrest

Philip Braham *(1838-1905)*

Limehouse Blues
Show: Andre Charlot's Revue of
1924
Opened: January 1924
Lyrics by: Douglas Furber

Hoagy Carmichael *(1899-1981)*

Little Old Lady
Show: Show is On
Opened: December 1936
Lyrics by: Stanley Adams

George M. Cohan *(1878-1942)*

Forty-Five Minutes from Broadway
Show: Forty-Five Minutes from
Broadway
Opened: January 1906
Lyrics by: George M. Cohan

Give My Regards to Broadway
Show: Little Johnny Jones
Opened: November 1904
Lyrics by: George M. Cohan .

Harrigan
Show: Fifty Miles from Boston
Opened: February 1908
Lyrics by: George M. Cohan

Mary's a Grand Old Name
Show: Forty-Five Minutes from
Broadway
Opened: January 1906
Lyrics by: George M. Cohan

George M. Cohan (continued)

Molly Malone
Show: Merry Malones
Opened: September 1927
Lyrics by: George M. Cohan

Yankee Doodle Boy
Show: Little Johnny Jones
Opened: November 1904
Lyrics by: George M. Cohan

You're a Grand Old Flag
Show: George Washington Jr.
Opened: February 1906
Lyrics by: George M. Cohan

Cy Coleman *(1929-)*

Big Spender
Show: Sweet Charity
Opened: January 1966
Lyrics by: Dorothy Fields

Hey, Look Me Over
Show: Wildcat
Opened: December 1960
Lyrics by: Carolyn Leigh

If My Friends Could See Me Now
Show: Sweet Charity
Opened: January 1966
Lyrics by: Dorothy Fields

Real Live Girl
Show: Little Me
Opened: November 1962
Lyrics by: Carolyn Leigh

Noël Coward *(1899-1973)*

I'll See You Again
Show: Bitter Sweet
Opened: November 1929
Lyrics by: Noël Coward

Ziguener
Show: Bitter Sweet
Opened: November 1929
Lyrics by: Noël Coward

B.G. (Buddy) DeSylva *(1896-1950)*

Cloe
Show: Sinbad
Opened: February 1918
Lyrics by: B.G. DeSylva

Walter Donaldson *(1893-1947)*

Love Me or Leave Me
Show: Whoopee
Opened: December 1928
Lyrics by: Gus Kahn

Makin' Whoopee
Show: Whoopee
Opened: December 1928
Lyrics by: Gus Kahn

Ervin Drake *(1919-)*

A Room Without Windows
Show: What Makes Sammy Run?
Opened: February 1964
Lyrics by: Ervin Drake

Vernon Duke *(1903-1969)*

April in Paris
Show: Walk a Little Faster
Opened: December 1932
Lyrics by: E.Y. Harburg

Cabin in the Sky
Show: Cabin in the Sky
Opened: October 1940
Lyrics by: John Latouche

I Can't Get Started
Show: Ziegfeld Follies
Opened: January 1935
Lyrics by: E.Y. Harburg

I Like the Likes of You
Show: Ziegfeld Follies
Opened: January 1934
Lyrics by: E.Y. Harburg

Taking a Chance on Love
Show: Cabin in the Sky
Opened: October 1940
Lyrics by: Ted Fetter

<u>Vernon Duke</u> (continued)
> **What is There to Say?**
> *Show:* Ziegfeld Follies
> *Opened:* January 1934
> *Lyrics by:* E.Y. Harburg

<u>Rudolf Friml</u> *(1897-1972)*
> **Giannina Mia**
> *Show:* Firefly
> *Opened:* December 1912
> *Lyrics by:* Otto Hauerbach
> (Harbach)

> **Indian Love Call**
> *Show:* Rose-Marie
> *Opened:* September 1924
> *Lyrics by:* Otto Harbach &
> Oscar Hammerstein II

> **Love is Like a Firefly**
> *Show:* Firefly
> *Opened:* December 1912
> *Lyrics by:* Otto Hauerbach
> (Harbach)

> **Only a Rose**
> *Show:* Vagabond King
> *Opened:* September 1925
> *Lyrics by:* Brian Hooker & W.H.
> Post

> **Rose-Marie**
> *Show:* Rose-Marie
> *Opened:* September 1924
> *Lyrics by:* Otto Harbach &
> Oscar Hammerstin II

> **Some Day**
> *Show:* Vagabond King
> *Opened:* September 1925
> *Lyrics by:* Brian Hooker & W.H.
> Post

> **Song of the Vagabonds**
> *Show:* Vagabond King
> *Opened:* September 1925
> *Lyrics by:* Brian Hooker & W.H.
> Post

<u>Rudolf Friml</u> (continued)
> **Sympathy**
> *Show:* Firefly
> *Opened:* December 1912
> *Lyrics by:* Otto Hauerbach
> (Harbach)

> **Totem Tom-Tom**
> *Show:* Rose-Marie
> *Opened:* September 1924
> *Lyrics by:* Otto Harbach &
> Oscar Hammerstein II

<u>Ed Gallagher</u>
> **Mr. Gallagher and Mr. Shean**
> *Show:* Ziegfeld Follies of 1922
> *Opened:* June 1922
> *Lyrics by:* Al Shean & Ernest
> Ball

<u>Percy Gaunt</u> *(1852-1896)*
> **After the Ball**
> *Show:* A Trip to Chinatown
> *Opened:* November 1891
> *Lyrics by:* Charles Harris

> **The Bowery**
> *Show:* A Trip to Chinatown
> *Opened:* November 1891
> *Lyrics by:* Percy Gaunt

<u>Gary Geld</u> *(1935-)*
> **Freedom**
> *Show:* Shenandoah
> *Opened:* January 1975
> *Lyrics by:* Peter Udell

<u>George Gershwin</u> *(1898-1937)*
> **Bess, You is My Woman Now**
> *Show:* Porgy and Bess
> *Opened:* October 1935
> *Lyrics by:* Ira Gershwin

> **Bidin' My Time**
> *Show:* Girl Crazy
> *Opened:* October 1930
> *Lyrics by:* Ira Gershwin

George Gershwin (continued)
But Not for Me
Show: Girl Crazy
Opened: October 1930
Lyrics by: Ira Gershwin

Clap Yo' Hands
Show: Oh, Kay!
Opened: November 1926
Lyrics by: Ira Gershwin

Could You Use Me?
Show: Girl Crazy
Opened: October 1930
Lyrics by: Ira Gershwin

Embraceable You
Show: Girl Crazy
Opened: October 1930
Lyrics by: Ira Gershwin

Fascinating Rhythm
Show: Lady, Be Good!
Opened: December 1924
Lyrics by: Ira Gershwin

Feeling I'm Falling
Show: Strike Up the Band
Opened: November 1928
Lyrics by: Ira Gershwin

Funny Face
Show: Funny Face
Opened: November 1927
Lyrics by: Ira Gershwin

He Loves and She Loves
Show: Funny Face
Opened: November 1927
Lyrics by: Ira Gershwin

How Long Has This Been Going On?
Show: Rosalie
Opened: January 1928
Lyrics by: Ira Gershwin

George Gershwin (continued)
I Got Plenty of Nothin'
Show: Porgy and Bess
Opened: October 1935
Lyrics by: DuBose Heyward & Ira Gershwin

I Got Rythm
Show: Girl Crazy
Opened: October 1930
Lyrics by: Ira Gershwin

I Loves You, Porgy
Show: Porgy and Bess
Opened: October 1935
Lyrics by: Ira Gershwin

I'll Build a Stairway to Paradise
Show: George White's Scandals (4th Edition)
Opened: August 1922
Lyrics by: B.G. DaSylva & Arthur Francis (Ira Gershwin)

I've Got A Crush on You
Show: Strike Up the Band
Opened: January 1930
Lyrics by: Ira Gershwin

It Ain't Necessarily So
Show: Porgy and Bess
Opened: October 1935
Lyrics by: Ira Gershwin

Liza
Show: Show Girl
Opened: July 1929
Lyrics by: Ira Gershwin

Love is Sweeping the Country
Show: Of Thee I Sing
Opened: December 1931
Lyrics by: Ira Gershwin

Maybe
Show: Oh, Kay!
Opened: November 1926
Lyrics by: Ira Gershwin

George Gershwin (continued)

Oh! Lady Be Good
Show: Lady, Be Good!
Opened: December 1924
Lyrics by: Ira Gershwin

Rhapsody in Blue
Show: George White's
　　　　Scandals (8th Edition)
Opened: June 1926
Lyrics by:

'S Wonderful
Show: Funny Face
Opened: November 1927
Lyrics by: Ira Gershwin

Somebody Loves Me
Show: George White's
　　　　Scandals (6th Edition)
Opened: June 1924
Lyrics by: B.G. DaSylva &
　　　　Ballard Macdonald

Someone to Watch Over Me
Show: Oh, Kay!
Opened: November 1926
Lyrics by: Ira Gershwin

Soon
Show: Strike Up the Band
Opened: January 1930
Lyrics by: Ira Gershwin

Strike Up the Band
Show: Strike Up the Band
Opened: January 1930
Lyrics by: Ira Gershwin

Summertime
Show: Porgy and Bess
Opened: October 1935
Lyrics by: DuBose Heyward

There's a Boat dat's Leavin' Soon for New York
Show: Porgy and Bess
Opened: October 1935
Lyrics by: Ira Gershwin

George Gershwin (continued)

Treat Me Rough
Show: Girl Crazy
Opened: October 1930
Lyrics by: Ira Gershwin

Who Cares?
Show: Of Thee I Sing
Opened: December 1931
Lyrics by: Ira Gershwin

Wintergreen for President
Show: Of Thee I Sing
Opened: December 1931
Lyrics by: Ira Gershwin

Jay Gorney *(1896-1990)*

Brother Can You Spare a Dime?
Show: Americana
Opened: October 1932
Lyrics by: E.Y. Harburg

Edvard Grieg *(1843-1907)*

Freddy and His Fiddle
Show: Song of Norway
Opened: August 1944
Lyrics by: Robert Wright &
　　　　George Forrest

I Love You
Show: Song of Norway
Opened: August 1944
Lyrics by: Robert Wright &
　　　　George Forrest

Midsummer's Eve
Show: Song of Norway
Opened: August 1944
Lyrics by: Robert Wright &
　　　　George Forrest

Strange Music
Show: Song of Norway
Opened: August 1944
Lyrics by: Robert Wright &
　　　　George Forrest

Manos Hadjidakis *(1925-)*

Never on Sunday
Show: Illya Darling
Opened: April 1967
Lyrics by. Joe Darion

Albert Hague *(1920-)*

Young and Foolish
Show: Plain and Fancy
Opened: January 1955
Lyrics by. Arnold Horwitt

Marvin Hamlisch *(1944-)*

One
Show: Chorus Line
Opened: April 1975
Lyrics by. Edward Kleban

What I Did for Love
Show: Chorus Line
Opened: April 1975
Lyrics by. Edward Kleban

James Hanley *(1892-1942)*

Second Hand Rose
Show: Ziegfeld Follies
Opened: June 1921
Lyrics by. Grant Clarke

Ray Henderson *(1896-1971)*

The Best Things in Life Are Free
Show: Good News!
Opened: September 1927
Lyrics by. B.G. DeSylva and Lew Brown

Birth of the Blues
Show: George White's
     Scandals (8th Edition)
Opened: June 1926
Lyrics by. B.G. DeSylva and Lew Brown

Ray Henderson (continued)

Black Bottom
Show: George White's
     Scandals (8th Edition)
Opened: June 1926
Lyrics by. B.G. DeSylva and Lew Brown

Button Up Your Overcoat
Show: Follow Thru
Opened: January 1929
Lyrics by. B.G. DeSylva and Lew Brown

Good News
Show: Good News!
Opened: September 1927
Lyrics by. B.G. DeSylva and Lew Brown

It All Depends on You
Show: Big Boy
Opened: January 1925
Lyrics by. Lew Brown

Life is Just a Bowl of Cherries
Show: George White's
     Scandals (11th Edition)
Opened: September 1931
Lyrics by. Lew Brown

Lucky in Love
Show: Good News!
Opened: September 1927
Lyrics by. B.G. DeSylva and Lew Brown

My Song
Show: George White's
     Scandals (11th Edition)
Opened: September 1931
Lyrics by. Lew Brown

Strike Me Pink
Show: Strike Me Pink
Opened: March 1933
Lyrics by. Lew Brown

Ray Henderson (continued)

Thank Your Father
Show: Flying High
Opened: March 1930
Lyrics by. B.G. DeSylva and Lew Brown

That's Why Darkies Were Born
Show: George White's
        Scandals (11th Edition)
Opened: September 1931
Lyrics by. Lew Brown

This is the Missus
Show: George White's
        Scandals (11th Edition)
Opened: September 1931
Lyrics by. Lew Brown

The Thrill is Gone
Show: George White's
        Scandals (11th Edition)
Opened: September 1931
Lyrics by. Lew Brown

Varsity Drag
Show: Good News!
Opened: September 1927
Lyrics by. B.G. DeSylva and Lew Brown

You're the Cream in My Coffee
Show: Hold Everything
Opened: October 1928
Lyrics by. B.G. DeSylva and Lew Brown

Victor Herbert *(1859-1924)*

Ah! Sweet Mystery of Life
Show: Naughty Marietta
Opened: November 1910
Lyrics by. Rida Johnson Young

Because You're You
Show: Red Mill
Opened: September 1906
Lyrics by

Victor Herbert (continued)

Every Day is Ladies' Day with Me
Show: Red Mill
Opened: September 1906
Lyrics by. Henry Blossom

Gypsy Love Song
Show: Fortune Teller
Opened: September 1928
Lyrics by. Harry B.Smith

I Can't Do the Sum
Show: Babes in Toyland
Opened: October 1903
Lyrics by. Glen MacDonough

I Want What I Want When I Want It
Show: Mlle. Modiste
Opened: December 1905
Lyrics by. Henry Blossom

I'm Falling in Love with Someone
Show: Naughty Marietta
Opened: November 1910
Lyrics by. Rida Johnson Young

Kiss in the Dark
Show: Orange Blossoms
Opened: September 1922
Lyrics by. B.G.DeSylva

Kiss Me Again
Show: Mlle. Modiste
Opened: December 1905
Lyrics by. Henry Blossom

March of the Toys
Show: Babes in Toyland
Opened: October 1903
Lyrics by. Glen MacDonough

'Neath the Southern Moon
Show: Naughty Marietta
Opened: November 1910

Victor Herbert (continued)
Neopolitan Love Song
Show: Princess Pat
Opened: September 1915
Lyrics by: Henry Blossom

Sweethearts
Show: Sweethearts
Opened: September 1913
Lyrics by: Robert B.Smith

Toyland
Show: Babes in Toyland
Opened: October 1903
Lyrics by: Glen MacDonough

Tramp! Tramp! Tramp!
Show: Naughty Marietta
Opened: November 1910
Lyrics by: Rida Johnson Young

Jerry Herman *(1933-)*
The Best of Times
Show: La Cage Aux Folles
Opened: August 1983
Lyrics by: Harvey Fierstein

Hello, Dolly!
Show: Hello, Dolly!
Opened: January 1964
Lyrics by: Jerry Herman

If He Walked Into My Life
Show: Mame
Opened: May 1966
Lyrics by: Jerry Herman

It Only Takes a Moment
Show: Hello, Dolly!
Opened: January 1964
Lyrics by: Jerry Herman

Mame
Show: Mame
Opened: May 1966
Lyrics by: Jerry Herman

Jerry Herman (continued)
Milk and Honey
Show: Milk and Honey
Opened: October 1961
Lyrics by: Jerry Herman

My Best Girl
Show: Mame
Opened: May 1966
Lyrics by: Jerry Herman

Ribbons Down My Back
Show: Hello, Dolly!
Opened: January 1964
Lyrics by: Jerry Herman

Shalom
Show: Milk and Honey
Opened: October 1961
Lyrics by: Jerry Herman

We Need a Little Christmas
Show: Mame
Opened: May 1966
Lyrics by: Jerry Herman

Karl Hoschna *(1877-1911)*
**Cuddle Up a Little Closer
Lovey Mine**
Show: Three Twins
Opened: June 1908
Lyrics by: Otto Harbach

Every Little Movement
Show: Madame Sherry
Opened: August 1910
Lyrics by: Otto Harbach

Girl of My Dreams
Show: Girl of My Dreams
Opened: August 1911
Lyrics by: Otto Harbach

Emmerich Kalman *(1882-1953)*
Play, Gypsies--Dance, Gypsies
Show: Countess Maritza
Opened: September 1926
Lyrics by: Harry Smith

John Kander *(1927-)*

Cabaret
Show: Cabaret
Opened: November 1966
Lyrics by. Fred Ebb

Jerome Kern *(1885-1945)*

All in Fun
Show: Very Warm for May
Opened: November 1939
Lyrics by. Oscar Hammerstein II

All the Things You Are
Show: Very Warm for May
Opened: November 1939
Lyrics by. Oscar Hammerstein II

Bill
Show: Showboat
Opened: December 1927
Lyrics by. Oscar Hammerstein II
     & P.G. Wodehouse

Can't Help Lovin' Dat Man
Show: Showboat
Opened: December 1927
Lyrics by. Oscar Hammerstein II

Don't Ever Leave Me
Show: Sweet Adeline
Opened: September 1929
Lyrics by. Oscar Hammerstein II

I've Told Every Little Star
Show: Music in the Air
Opened: November 1932
Lyrics by. Oscar Hammerstein II

Life Upon the Wicked Stage
Show: Showboat
Opened: December 1927
Lyrics by. Oscar Hammerstein II

Look for the Silver Lining
Show: Sally
Opened: December 1920
Lyrics by. B.G. DeSylva

Jerome Kern (continued)

Make Believe
Show: Showboat
Opened: December 1927
Lyrics by. Oscar Hammerstein II

The Night Was Made for Love
Show: Cat and the Fiddle
Opened: October 1931
Lyrics by. Otto Harbach

Ol' Man River
Show: Showboat
Opened: December 1927
Lyrics by. Oscar Hammerstein II

She Didn't Say "Yes"
Show: Cat and the Fiddle
Opened: October 1931
Lyrics by. Otto Harbach

Smoke Gets in our Eyes
Show: Roberta
Opened: November 1933
Lyrics by. Otto Harbach

The Song is You
Show: Music in the Air
Opened: November 1932
Lyrics by. Oscar Hammerstein II

Sunny
Show: Sunny
Opened: September 1925
Lyrics by. Otto Harbach & Oscar
     Hammerstein II

They Didn't Believe Me
Show: Girl from Utah
Opened: August 1914
Lyrics by. Herbert Reynolds

Till the Clouds Roll By
Show: Oh, Boy!
Opened: February 1917
Lyrics by. P.G. Wodehouse

Jerome Kern (continued)

The Touch of Your Hand
Show: Roberta
Opened: November 1933
Lyrics by. Otto Harbach

Who?
Show: Sunny
Opened: September 1925
Lyrics by. Otto Harbach & Oscar
    Hammerstein II

Why Do I Love You?
Show: Showboat
Opened: December 1927
Lyrics by. Oscar Hammerstein II

Why Was I Born?
Show: Sweet Adeline
Opened: September 1929
Lyrics by. Oscar Hammerstein II

Yesterdays
Show: Roberta
Opened: November 1933
Lyrics by. Otto Harbach

You Are Love
Show: Showboat
Opened: December 1927
Lyrics by. Oscar Hammerstein II

You're Devastating
Show: Roberta
Opened: November 1933
Lyrics by. Otto Harbach

Burton Lane *(1912-)*

How Are Things in Glocca Morra?
Show: Finian's Rainbow
Opened: January 1947
Lyrics by. E.Y. Harburg

If This Isn't Love
Show: Finian's Rainbow
Opened: January 1947
Lyrics by. E.Y. Harburg

Burton Lane (continued)

Look to the Rainbow
Show: Finian's Rainbow
Opened: January 1947
Lyrics by. E.Y. Harburg

Old Devil Moon
Show: Finian's Rainbow
Opened: January 1947
Lyrics by. E.Y. Harburg

On a Clear Day
Show: On a Clear Day You Can
    See Forever
Opened: October 1965
Lyrics by. Alan Jay Lerner

That Great Come-and-Get-It Day
Show: Finian's Rainbow
Opened: January 1947
Lyrics by. E.Y. Harburg

There's a Great Day Coming Manana
Show: Hold On to Your Hats
Opened: September 1940
Lyrics by. E.Y. Harburg

What Did I Have That I Don't Have?
Show: On a Clear Day You Can
    See Forever
Opened: October 1965
Lyrics by. Alan Jay Lerner

When I'm Not Near the Girl I Love
Show: Finian's Rainbow
Opened: January 1947
Lyrics by. E.Y. Harburg

The World in My Arms
Show: Hold On to Your Hats
Opened: September 1940
Lyrics by. E.Y. Harburg

Mitch Leigh *(1928-)*

Impossible Dream (The Quest)
Show: Man of La Mancha
Opened: November 1965
Lyrics by: Joe Darion

Man of La Mancha (I, Don Quixote)
Show: Man of La Mancha
Opened: November 1965
Lyrics by: Joe Darion

Richard Lewine *(1910-)*

Saturday Night in Cental Park
Show: Make Mine Manhattan
Opened: January 1948
Lyrics by: Arnold Horwitt

Andrew Lloyd Webber *(1948-)*

Don't Cry for Me, Argentina
Show: Evita
Opened: September 1979
Lyrics by: Tim Rice

I Don't Know How to Love Him
Show: Jesus Christ Superstar
Opened: October 1971
Lyrics by: Tim Rice

Memory
Show: Cats
Opened: October 1982
Lyrics by: T.S. Eliot

Music of the Night
Show: Phantom of the Opera
Opened: January 1988
Lyrics by: Charles Hart

Superstar
Show: Jesus Christ Superstar
Opened: October 1971
Lyrics by: Tim Rice

Frank Loesser *(1910-1969)*

Big "D"
Show: Most Happy Fella
Opened: May 1956
Lyrics by: Frank Loesser

Brotherhood of Man
Show: How to Succeed in Business Without Really Trying
Opened: October 1961
Lyrics by: Frank Loesser

Bushel and a Peck
Show: Guys and Dolls
Opened: November 1950
Lyrics by: Frank Loesser

Company Way
Show: How to Succeed in Business Without Really Trying
Opened: October 1961
Lyrics by: Frank Loesser

Guys and Dolls
Show: Guys and Dolls
Opened: November 1950
Lyrics by: Frank Loesser

I Believe in You
Show: How to Succeed in Business Without Really Trying
Opened: October 1961
Lyrics by: Frank Loesser

I'll Know
Show: Guys and Dolls
Opened: November 1950
Lyrics by: Frank Loesser

I've Never Been in Love Before
Show: Guys and Dolls
Opened: November 1950
Lyrics by: Frank Loesser

Frank Loesser (continued)

If I Were a Bell
Show: Guys and Dolls
Opened: November 1950
Lyrics by: Frank Loesser

Luck Be a Lady
Show: Guys and Dolls
Opened: November 1950
Lyrics by: Frank Loesser

My Darling, My Darling
Show: Where's Charley?
Opened: October 1948
Lyrics by: Frank Loesser

Once in Love with Amy
Show: Where's Charley?
Opened: October 1948
Lyrics by: Frank Loesser

Sit Down You're Rockin' the Boat
Show: Guys and Dolls
Opened: November 1950
Lyrics by: Frank Loesser

Standing on the Corner
Show: Most Happy Fella
Opened: May 1956
Lyrics by: Frank Loesser

Summertime Love
Show: Greenwillow
Opened: March 1960
Lyrics by: Frank Loesser

Frederick Loewe *(1904-1988)*

Almost Like Being in Love
Show: Brigadoon
Opened: March 1947
Lyrics by: Alan Jay Lerner

Camelot
Show: Camelot
Opened: December 1960
Lyrics by: Alan Jay Lerner

Frederick Loewe (continued)

Come to Me, Bend to Me
Show: Brigadoon
Opened: March 1947
Lyrics by: Alan Jay Lerner

Follow Me
Show: Camelot
Opened: December 1960
Lyrics by: Alan Jay Lerner

Get Me to the Church on Time
Show: My Fair Lady
Opened: March 1956
Lyrics by: Alan Jay Lerner

Heather on the Hill
Show: Brigadoon
Opened: March 1947
Lyrics by: Alan Jay Lerner

How to Handle a Woman
Show: Camelot
Opened: December 1960
Lyrics by: Alan Jay Lerner

I Could Have Danced All Night
Show: My Fair Lady
Opened: March 1956
Lyrics by: Alan Jay Lerner

I Loved You Once in Silence
Show: Camelot
Opened: December 1960
Lyrics by: Alan Jay Lerner

I Talk to the Trees
Show: Paint Your Wagon
Opened: November 1951
Lyrics by: Alan Jay Lerner

I've Grown Accustomed to Her Face
Show: My Fair Lady
Opened: March 1956
Lyrics by: Alan Jay Lerner

Frederick Loewe (continued)

If Ever I Would Leave You
Show: Camelot
Opened: December 1960
Lyrics by: Alan Jay Lerner

Just You Wait
Show: My Fair Lady
Opened: March 1956
Lyrics by: Alan Jay Lerner

On the Street Where You Live
Show: My Fair Lady
Opened: March 1956
Lyrics by: Alan Jay Lerner

The Rain in Spain
Show: My Fair Lady
Opened: March 1956
Lyrics by: Alan Jay Lerner

There But for You Go I
Show: Brigadoon
Opened: March 1947
Lyrics by: Alan Jay Lerner

They Call the Wind Maria
Show: Paint Your Wagon
Opened: November 1951
Lyrics by: Alan Jay Lerner

What Do the Simple Folk Do?
Show: Camelot
Opened: December 1960
Lyrics by: Alan Jay Lerner

With a Little Bit of Luck
Show: My Fair Lady
Opened: March 1956
Lyrics by: Alan Jay Lerner

Wouldn't It Be Loverly?
Show: My Fair Lady
Opened: March 1956
Lyrics by: Alan Jay Lerner

Galt MacDermot *(1928-)*

Aquarius
Show: Hair
Opened: April 1968
Lyrics by. Gerome Ragni &
James Rado

Let the Sunshine In
Show: Hair
Opened: April 1968
Lyrics by. Gerome Ragni &
James Rado

Hugh Martin *(1914-)*

Buckle Down Winsocki
Show: Best Foot Forward
Opened: October 1941
Lyrics by. Ralph Blane

What Do You Think I Am?
Show: Best Foot Forward
Opened: October 1941
Lyrics by. Ralph Blane

Jimmy McHugh *(1895-1969)*

Diga Diga Doo
Show: Blackbirds of 1928
Opened: May 1928
Lyrics by. Dorothy Fields

Exactly Like You
Show: International Revue
Opened: February 1930
Lyrics by. Dorothy Fields

I Can't Give You Anything But Love
Show: Blackbirds of 1928
Opened: May 1928
Lyrics by. Dorothy Fields

On the Sunny Side of the Street
Show: International Revue
Opened: February 1930
Lyrics by. Dorothy Fields

Bob Merrill *(1921-)*
Love Makes the World Go Round
Show: Carnival
Opened: April 1961
Lyrics by. Bob Merrill

Take Me Along
Show: Take Me Along
Opened: October 1959
Lyrics by. Bob Merrill

Joseph Meyer *(1884-1959)*
If You Knew Susie
Show: Big Boy
Opened: January 1925
Lyrics by. B.G. DeSylva

Anthony Newley *(1931-)*
Gonna Build a Mountain
Show: Stop the World -- I Want
    to Get Off
Opened: October 1962
Lyrics by. Leslie Bricusse

Once in a Lifetime
Show: Stop the World -- I Want
    to Get Off
Opened: October 1962
Lyrics by. Leslie Bricusse

What Kind of Fool Am I?
Show: Stop the World -- I Want
    to Get Off
Opened: October 1962
Lyrics by. Leslie Bricusse

Who Can I Turn To?
Show: Roar of the Greasepaint--
    The Smell of the Crowd
Opened: May 1965
Lyrics by. Leslie Bricusse

A Wonderful Day Like Today
Show: Roar of the Greasepaint--
    The Smell of the Crowd
Opened: May 1965
Lyrics by. Leslie Bricusse

Ray Noble *(1903-1978)*
Good Night, Sweetheart
Show: Earl Carroll Vanities
Opened: August 1927
Lyrics by. Peg Connelly

Ole Olsen *(1892-1963)*
**Oh! Gee, Oh! Gosh, Oh! Golly,
I'm in Love**
Show: Ziegfeld Follies of 1922
Opened: June 1922
Lyrics by. Chic Johnson &
    Ernest Brewer

Cole Porter *(1891-1964)*
All Through the Night
Show: Anything Goes
Opened: November 1934
Lyrics by. Cole Porter

**Always True to You in May
Fashion**
Show: Kiss Me Kate
Opened: December 1940
Lyrics by. Cole Porter

Another Op'nin, Another Show
Show: Kiss Me Kate
Opened: December 1940
Lyrics by. Cole Porter

Anything Goes
Show: Anything Goes
Opened: November 1934
Lyrics by. Cole Porter

At Long Last Love
Show: You Never Know
Opened: September 1938
Lyrics by. Cole Porter

Begin the Beguine
Show: Jubilee
Opened: October 1935
Lyrics by. Cole Porter

Cole Porter (continued)

Bianca
Show: Kiss Me Kate
Opened: December 1940
Lyrics by. Cole Porter

Blow, Gabriel, Blow
Show: Anything Goes
Opened: November 1934
Lyrics by. Cole Porter

Brush Up Your Shakespeare
Show: Kiss Me Kate
Opened: December 1940
Lyrics by. Cole Porter

C'est Magnifique
Show: Can-Can
Opened: May 1953
Lyrics by. Cole Porter

Do I Love You?
Show: Dubarry Was a Lady
Opened: December 1939
Lyrics by. Cole Porter

Ev'rytime We Say Goodbye
Show: Seven Lively Arts
Opened: December 1944
Lyrics by. Cole Porter

Friendship
Show: Dubarry Was a Lady
Opened: December 1939
Lyrics by. Cole Porter

Get Out of Town
Show: Leave It to Me
Opened: November 1938
Lyrics by. Cole Porter

Hey, Good Lookin'
Show: Something for the Boys
Opened: January 1943
Lyrics by. Cole Porter

I Get a Kick Out of You
Show: Anything Goes
Opened: November 1934
Lyrics by. Cole Porter

Cole Porter (continued)

I Love Paris
Show: Can-Can
Opened: May 1953
Lyrics by. Cole Porter

I Love You
Show: Mexican Hayride
Opened: January 1944
Lyrics by: Cole Porter

I'm in Love Again
Show: Greenwich Village Follies
(6th Edition)
Opened: September 1924
Lyrics by. Cole Porter

It's All Right with Me
Show: Can-Can
Opened: May 1953
Lyrics by. Cole Porter

It's De-Lovely
Show: Red, Hot and Blue!
Opened: October 1936
Lyrics by. Cole Porter

Just One of Those Things
Show: Jubilee
Opened: October 1935
Lyrics by. Cole Porter

Let's Be Buddies
Show: Panama Hattie
Opened: October 1940
Lyrics by. Cole Porter

Let's Do It
Show: Paris
Opened: October 1928
Lyrics by. Cole Porter

Let's Not Talk About Love
Show: Let's Face It!
Opened: October 1941
Lyrics by. Cole Porter

Cole Porter (continued)

Love for Sale
Show: New Yorkers
Opened: December 1930
Lyrics by. Cole Porter

My Heart Belongs to Daddy
Show: Leave It to Me
Opened: November 1938
Lyrics by. Cole Porter

Night and Day
Show: Gay Divorce
Opened: November 1932
Lyrics by. Cole Porter

Ridin' High
Show: Red, Hot and Blue!
Opened: October 1936
Lyrics by. Cole Porter

So in Love
Show: Kiss Me Kate
Opened: December 1940
Lyrics by. Cole Porter

Something for the Boys
Show: Something for the Boys
Opened: January 1943
Lyrics by. Cole Porter

That's All
Show: Silk Stockings
Opened: February 1955
Lyrics by. Cole Porter

Too Darn Hot
Show: Kiss Me Kate
Opened: December 1940
Lyrics by. Cole Porter

Use Your Imagination
Show: Out of This World
Opened: December 1950
Lyrics by. Cole Porter

Cole Porter (continued)

We Open in Venice
Show: Kiss Me Kate
Opened: December 1940
Lyrics by. Cole Porter

Well, Did You Evah?
Show: DuBarry Was a Lady
Opened: December 1939
Lyrics by. Cole Porter

Were Thine That Special Face
Show: Kiss Me Kate
Opened: December 1940
Lyrics by. Cole Porter

What is This Thing Called Love?
Show: Wake Up and Dream
Opened: December 1929
Lyrics by. Cole Porter

Where is the Life That Late I Led?
Show: Kiss Me Kate
Opened: December 1940
Lyrics by. Cole Porter

Why Shouldn't I?
Show: Jubilee
Opened: October 1935
Lyrics by. Cole Porter

Why Can't You Behave?
Show: Kiss Me Kate
Opened: December 1940
Lyrics by. Cole Porter

Why Shouldn't I?
Show: Jubilee
Opened: October 1935
Lyrics by. Cole Porter

Wunderbar
Show: Kiss Me Kate
Opened: December 1940
Lyrics by. Cole Porter

Cole Porter (continued)

You Do Something to Me
Show: Fifty Million Frenchmen
Opened: November 1929
Lyrics by: Cole Porter

You're the Top
Show: Anything Goes
Opened: November 1934
Lyrics by: Cole Porter

Richard Rodgers *(1902-1979)*

All at Once
Show: Babes in Arms
Opened: April 1937
Lyrics by: Lorenz Hart

All At Once You Love Her
Show: Pipe Dream
Opened: November 1955
Lyrics by: Oscar Hammerstein II

All er Nothin'
Show: Oklahoma!
Opened: March 1943
Lyrics by: Oscar Hammerstein II

Bali Ha'i
Show: South Pacific
Opened: April 1949
Lyrics by: Oscar Hammerstein II

Bewitched, Bothered and Bewildered
Show: Pal Joey
Opened: December 1940
Lyrics by: Lorenz Hart

Bloody Mary
Show: South Pacific
Opened: April 1949
Lyrics by: Oscar Hammerstein II

The Blue Room
Show: The Girl Friend
Opened: March 1926
Lyrics by: Lorenz Hart

Richard Rodgers (continued)

Climb Ev'ry Mountain
Show: Sound of Music
Opened: November 1959
Lyrics by: Oscar Hammerstein II

A Cockeyed Optimist
Show: South Pacific
Opened: April 1949
Lyrics by: Oscar Hammerstein II

Dîtes-Moi
Show: South Pacific
Opened: April 1949
Lyrics by: Oscar Hammerstein II

Do I Hear a Waltz?
Show: Do I Hear a Waltz?
Opened: March 1965
Lyrics by: Stephen Sondheim

Do-Re-Mi
Show: Sound of Music
Opened: November 1959
Lyrics by: Oscar Hammerstein II

Edelweiss
Show: Sound of Music
Opened: November 1959
Lyrics by: Oscar Hammerstein II

Falling in Love With Love
Show: Boys from Syacuse
Opened: November 1938
Lyrics by: Lorenz Hart

A Fellow Needs a Girl
Show: Allegro
Opened: October 1947
Lyrics by: Oscar Hammerstein II

The Gentleman is a Dope
Show: Allegro
Opened: October 1947
Lyrics by: Oscar Hammerstein II

Getting to Know You
Show: King and I
Opened: March 1951
Lyrics by: Oscar Hammerstein II

Richard Rodgers (continued)

The Girl Friend
Show: The Girl Friend
Opened: March 1926
Lyrics by. Lorenz Hart

Happy Talk
Show: South Pacific
Opened: April 1949
Lyrics by. Oscar Hammerstein II

Have You Met Miss Jones?
Show: I'd Rather Be Right
Opened: November 1937
Lyrics by. Lorenz Hart

Hello, Young Lovers
Show: King and I
Opened: March 1951
Lyrics by. Oscar Hammerstein II

Honey Bun
Show: South Pacific
Opened: April 1949
Lyrics by. Oscar Hammerstein II

I Cain't Say No
Show: Oklahoma!
Opened: March 1943·
Lyrics by. Oscar Hammerstein II

I Could Write a Book
Show: Pal Joey
Opened: December 1940
Lyrics by. Lorenz Hart

I Didn't Know What Time It Was
Show: Too Many Girls
Opened: Ocatober 1939
Lyrics by. Lorenz Hart

I Enjoy Being a Girl
Show: Flower Drum Song
Opened: December 1958
Lyrics by. Oscar Hammerstein II

Richard Rodgers (continued)

I Have Dreamed
Show: King and I
Opened: March 1951
Lyrics by. Oscar Hammerstein

I Like to Recognize the Tune
Show: Too Many Girls
Opened: October 1939
Lyrics by. Lorenz Hart

I Married an Angel
Show: I Married an Angel
Opened: May 1938
Lyrics by. Lorenz Hart

I Whistle a Happy Tune
Show: King and I
Opened: March 1951
Lyrics by. Oscar Hammerstein II

I Wish I Were in Love Again
Show: Babes in Arms
Opened: April 1937
Lyrics by. Lorenz Hart

I'm Gonna Wash That Man Right Out of My Hair
Show: South Pacific
Opened: April 1949
Lyrics by. Oscar Hammerstein II

I've Got Five Dollars
Show: America's Sweetheart
Opened: February 1931
Lyrics by. Lorenz Hart

If I Loved You
Show: Carousel
Opened: April 1945
Lyrics by. Oscar Hammerstein II

It Never Entered My Mind
Show: Higher and Higher
Opened: April 1940
Lyrics by. Lorenz Hart

Richard Rodgers (continued)

Johnny One Note
Show: Babes in Arms
Opened: April 1937
Lyrics by: Lorenz Hart

June is Bustin' Out All Over
Show: Carousel
Opened: April 1945
Lyrics by: Oscar Hammerstein II

Kansas City
Show: Oklahoma!
Opened: March 1943
Lyrics by: Oscar Hammerstein II

The Lady is a Tramp
Show: Babes in Arms
Opened: April 1937
Lyrics by: Lorenz Hart

Little Girl Blue
Show: Jumbo
Opened: November 1935
Lyrics by: Lorenz Hart

Love, Look Away
Show: Flower Drum Song
Opened: December 1958
Lyrics by: Oscar Hammerstein II

Manhattan
Show: Garrick Gaieties
Opened: May 1925
Lyrics by: Lorenz Hart

Many a New Day
Show: Oklahoma!
Opened: March 1943
Lyrics by: Oscar Hammerstein II

Maria
Show: Sound of Music
Opened: November 1959
Lyrics by: Oscar Hammerstein II

Richard Rodgers (continued)

The Most Beautiful Girl in the World
Show: Jumbo
Opened: November 1935
Lyrics by: Lorenz Hart

Mountain Greenery
Show: Garrick Gaieties
Opened: May 1926
Lyrics by: Lorenz Hart

Mr. Snow
Show: Carousel
Opened: April 1945
Lyrics by: Oscar Hammerstein II

My Favorite Things
Show: Sound of Music
Opened: November 1959
Lyrics by: Oscar Hammerstein II

My Funny Valentine
Show: Babes in Arms
Opened: April 1937
Lyrics by: Lorenz Hart

My Heart Stood Still
Show: Connecticut Yankee
Opened: November 1927
Lyrics by: Lorenz Hart

My Romance
Show: Jumbo
Opened: November 1935
Lyrics by: Lorenz Hart

No Other Love
Show: Me and Juliet
Opened: May 1953
Lyrics by: Oscar Hammerstein II

Oh, What a Beautiful Mornin'
Show: Oklahoma!
Opened: March 1943
Lyrics by: Oscar Hammerstein II

Richard Rodgers (continued)

Oklahoma
Show: Oklahoma!
Opened: March 1943
Lyrics by: Oscar Hammerstein II

Out of My Dreams
Show: Oklahoma!
Opened: March 1943
Lyrics by: Oscar Hammerstein II

People Will Say We're in Love
Show: Oklahoma!
Opened: March 1943
Lyrics by: Oscar Hammerstein II

Pore Jud
Show: Oklahoma!
Opened: March 1943
Lyrics by: Oscar Hammerstein II

Quiet Night
Show: On Your Toes
Opened: April 1936
Lyrics by: Lorenz Hart

A Real Nice Clambake
Show: Carousel
Opened: April 1945
Lyrics by: Oscar Hammerstein II

Sentimental Me
Show: Garrick Gaieties
Opened: May 1925
Lyrics by: Lorenz Hart

Shall We Dance?
Show: King and I
Opened: March 1951
Lyrics by: Oscar Hammerstein II

Sing for Your Supper
Show: Boys from Syacuse
Opened: November 1938
Lyrics by: Lorenz Hart

Sixteen Going on Seventeen
Show: Sound of Music
Opened: November 1959
Lyrics by: Oscar Hammerstein II

Richard Rodgers (continued)

Slaughter on Tenth Avenue
Show: On Your Toes
Opened: April 1936
Lyrics by: (Instrumental)

So Far
Show: Allegro
Opened: October 1947
Lyrics by: Oscar Hammerstein II

So Long, Farewell
Show: Sound of Music
Opened: November 1959
Lyrics by: Oscar Hammerstein II

Soliloquy (Carousel)
Show: Carousel
Opened: April 1945
Lyrics by: Oscar Hammerstein II

Some Enchanted Evening
Show: South Pacific
Opened: April 1949
Lyrics by: Oscar Hammerstein II

Something Wonderful
Show: King and I
Opened: March 1951
Lyrics by: Oscar Hammerstein II

The Sound of Music
Show: Sound of Music
Opened: November 1959
Lyrics by: Oscar Hammerstein II

Spring is Here
Show: I Married an Angel
Opened: May 1938
Lyrics by: Lorenz Hart

The Surrey With the Fringe on Top
Show: Oklahoma!
Opened: March 1943
Lyrics by: Oscar Hammerstein II

Richard Rodgers (continued)

Sweetest Sounds
Show: No Strings
Opened: March 1962
Lyrics by: Richard Rodgers

Ten Cents a Dance
Show: Simple Simon
Opened: February 1930
Lyrics by: Lorenz Hart

There is Nothin' Like a Dame
Show: South Pacific
Opened: April 1949
Lyrics by: Oscar Hammerstein II

There's a Small Hotel
Show: On Your Toes
Opened: April 1936
Lyrics by: Lorenz Hart

This Can't Be Love
Show: Boys from Syacuse
Opened: November 1938
Lyrics by: Lorenz Hart

This Nearly Was Mine
Show: South Pacific
Opened: April 1949
Lyrics by: Oscar Hammerstein II

Thou Swell
Show: Connecticut Yankee
Opened: November 1927
Lyrics by: Lorenz Hart

Wait Till You See Her
Show: By Jupiter
Opened: November 1938
Lyrics by: Lorenz Hart

We Kiss in a Shadow
Show: King and I
Opened: March 1951
Lyrics by: Oscar Hammerstein II

Richard Rodgers (continued)

What's the Use of Wond'rin'
Show: Carousel
Opened: April 1945
Lyrics by: Oscar Hammerstein II

Where or When
Show: Babes in Arms
Opened: April 1937
Lyrics by: Lorenz Hart

With a Song in My Hert
Show: Spring is Here
Opened: March 1929
Lyrics by: Lorenz Hart

A Wonderful Guy
Show: South Pacific
Opened: April 1949
Lyrics by: Oscar Hammerstein II

You Are Beautiful
Show: Flower Drum Song
Opened: December 1958
Lyrics by: Oscar Hammerstein II

You Are Never Away
Show: Allegro
Opened: October 1947
Lyrics by: Oscar Hammerstein II

You Took Advantage of Me
Show: Present Arms
Opened: April 1928
Lyrics by: Lorenz Hart

You'll Never Walk Alone
Show: Carousel
Opened: April 1945
Lyrics by: Oscar Hammerstein II

You've Got to Be Carefully Taught
Show: South Pacific
Opened: April 1949
Lyrics by: Oscar Hammerstein II

Richard Rodgers (continued)
Younger Than Springtime
Show: South Pacific
Opened: April 1949
Lyrics by. Oscar Hammerstein II

Sigmund Romberg *(1887-1951)*
Auf Wiedersehn
Show: Blue Paradise
Opened: August 1915
Lyrics by. Herbert Reynolds

Close As Pages in a Book
Show: Up in Central Park
Opened: January 1945
Lyrics by. Dorothy Fields

Deep in My Heart Dear
Show: Student Prince in
   Heidelberg
Opened: December 1924
Lyrics by. Dorothy Donnelly

Desert Song
Show: Desert Song
Opened: November 1926
Lyrics by. Otto Harbach &
   Oscar Hammerstein II

Drinking Song
Show: Student Prince in
   Heidelberg
Opened: December 1924
Lyrics by. Dorothy Donnelly

Golden Days
Show: Student Prince in
   Heidelberg
Opened: December 1924
Lyrics by. Dorothy Donnelly

**It Doesn't Cost You Anything
to Dream**
Show: Up in Central Park
Opened: January 1945
Lyrics by. Dorothy Fields

Sigmund Romberg (continued)
Lover, Come Back to Me
Show: New Moon
Opened: September 1928
Lyrics by. Oscar Hammerstein II

One Alone
Show: Desert Song
Opened: November 1926
Lyrics by. Otto Harbach & Oscar
   Hammerstein II

One Kiss
Show: New Moon
Opened: September 1928
Lyrics by. Oscar Hammerstein II

Riff Song
Show: Desert Song
Opened: November 1926
Lyrics by. Otto Harbach & Oscar
   Hammerstein II

Romance
Show: Desert Song
Opened: November 1926
Lyrics by. Otto Harbach& Oscar
   Hammerstein II

Softly, As in a Morning Sunrise
Show: New Moon
Opened: September 1928
Lyrics by. Oscar Hammerstein II

Stouthearted Men
Show: New Moon
Opened: September 1928
Lyrics by. Oscar Hammerstein II

Wanting You
Show: New Moon
Opened: September 1928
Lyrics by. Oscar Hammerstein II

Will You Remember?
Show: Maytime
Opened: August 1917
Lyrics by. Rida Johnson Young

Sigmund Romberg (continued)

Your Land and My Land
Show: My Maryland
Opened: September 1927
Lyrics by: Dorothy Donnelly

Harold Rome *(1908-)*

F.D.R. Jones
Show: Sing Out the News
Opened: September 1928
Lyrics by: Harold Rome

Fanny
Show: Fanny
Opened: November 1954
Lyrics by: Harold Rome

Have I Told You Lately?
Show: I Can Get It For You
    Wholesale
Opened: March 1962
Lyrics by: Harold Rome

Pocketful of Dreams
Show: Michael Todd's Peep
    Show
Opened: June 1950
Lyrics by: Harold Rome

South America, Take It Away
Show: Call Me Mister
Opened: April 1946
Lyrics by: Harold Rome

Wish You Were Here
Show: Wish You Were Here
Opened: June 1952
Lyrics by: Harold Rome

Harvey Schmidt *(1929-)*

My Cup Runneth Over
Show: I Do! I Do!
Opened: December 1966
Lyrics by: Tom Jones

Soon It's Gonna Rain
Show: Fantasticks
Opened: May 1960
Lyrics by: Tom Jones

Harvey Schmidt (continued)

Try to Remember
Show: Fantasticks
Opened: May 1960
Lyrics by: Tom Jones

Arthur Schwartz *(1900-1984)*

Alone Together
Show: Flying Colors
Opened: September 1932
Lyrics by: Howard Dietz

Dancing in the Dark
Show: Band Wagon
Opened: June 1931
Lyrics by: Howard Dietz

**I Guess I'll Have to Change
My Plans**
Show: Little Show
Opened: April 1929
Lyrics by: Howard Dietz

I Love Louisa
Show: Band Wagon
Opened: Juen 1931
Lyrics by: Howard Dietz

I See Your Face Before Me
Show: Between the Devil
Opened: December 1937
Lyrics by: Howard Dietz

**If There is Someone Lovelier
Than You**
Show: Revenge with Music
Opened: November 1934
Lyrics by: Howard Dietz

Louisiana Hayride
Show: Flying Colors
Opened: September 1932
Lyrics by: Howard Dietz

New Sun in the Sky
Show: Band Wagon
Opened: June 1931
Lyrics by: Howard Dietz

Arthur Schwartz (continued)
Rhode Island is Famous for You
Show: Inside U.S.A.
Opened: April 1948
Lyrics by. Howard Dietz

A Shine on Your Shoes
Show: Flying Colors
Opened: September 1932
Lyrics by. Howard Dietz

Something to Remember You By
Show: Three's a Crowd
Opened: October 1930
Lyrics by. Howard Dietz

You and the Night and the Music
Show: Revenge with Music
Opened: November 1934
Lyrics by. Howard Dietz

Jean Schwartz *(1878-1956)*
Rock-a-Bye Your Baby With a Dixie Melody
Show: Sinbad
Opened: February 1918
Lyrics by. Sam Lewis & Joe Young

Stephen Schwartz *(1948-)*
Day by Day
Show: Godspell
Opened: May 1971
Lyrics by. John-Michael Tebelak

Mark Sharlap
I Gotta Crow
Show: Peter Pan
Opened: Octrober 1954
Lyrics by. Carolyn Leigh

Louis Silvers *(1889-1964)*
April Showers
Show: Bombo
Opened: October 1921
Lyrics by. B.G. DeSylva

Stephen Sondheim *(1930-)*
Comedy Tonight
Show: Funny Thing Happened on the Way to the Forum
Opened: May 1962
Lyrics by. Stephen Sondheim

Send in the Clowns
Show: A Little Night Music
Opened: February 1973
Lyrics by. Hugh Wheeler

Sam Stept *(1897-1964)*
Comes Love
Show: Yokel Boy
Opened: July 1939
Lyrics by. Lew Brown & Charles Tobias

Oscar Straus *(1870-1954)*
My Hero
Show: Chocolate Soldier
Opened: September 1909
Lyrics by. Stanislaus Stange

Sympathy
Show: Chocolate Soldier
Opened: September 1909
Lyrics by. Stanislaus Stange

Charles Strouse *(1928-)*
Kids
Show: Bye Bye Birdie
Opened: April 1960
Lyrics by. Lee Adams

A Lot of Livin' to Do
Show: Bye Bye Birdie
Opened: April 1960
Lyrics by. Lee Adams

Charles Strouse (continued)

Once Upon a Time
Show: All American
Opened: March 1962
Lyrics by. Lee Adams

Put on a Happy Face
Show: Bye Bye Birdie
Opened: April 1960
Lyrics by. Lee Adams

Tomorrow
Show: Annie
Opened: April 1977
Lyrics by. Martin Charnin

Leslie Stuart (d. 1928)

Tell Me Pretty Maiden
Show: Florodora
Opened: November 1900`
Lyrics by. Leslie Stuart

Jule Styne (1905-)

All I Need is the Girl
Show: Gypsy
Opened: May 1959
Lyrics by. Stephen Sondheim

Be a Santa
Show: Subways Are For
            Sleeping
Opened: December 1961
Lyrics by. Adolph Green & Betty
            Comden

Bye, Bye, Baby
Show: Gentlemen Prefer
            Blondes
Opened: December 1949
Lyrics by. Leo Robin

Comes Once in a Lifetime
Show: Subways Are For
            Sleeping
Opened: December 1961
Lyrics by. Adolph Green & Betty
            Comden

Jule Styne (continued)

Cry Like the Wind
Show: Do Re Mi
Opened: December 1960
Lyrics by. Adolph Green & Betty
            Comden

Diamonds Are a Girl's Best Friend
Show: Gentlemen Prefer
            Blondes
Opened: December 1949
Lyrics by. Leo Robin

Don't Rain on My Parade
Show: Funny Girl
Opened: March 1964
Lyrics by. Bob Merrill

Everything's Coming Up Roses
Show: Gypsy
Opened: May 1959
Lyrics by. Stephen Sondheim

How Do You Speak to an Angel?
Show: Hazel Flagg
Opened: February 1953
Lyrics by. Bob Hilliard

I Still Get Jealous
Show: High Button Shoes
Opened: October 1947
Lyrics by. Sammy Cahn

Just in Time
Show: Bells are Ringing
Opened: November 1956
Lyrics by. Adoph Green & Betty
            Comden

Let Me Entertain You
Show: Gypsy
Opened: May 1959
Lyrics by. Stephen Sondheim

Jule Styne (continued)
Little Lamb
Show: Gypsy
Opened: May 1959
Lyrics by: Stephen Sondheim

Make Someone Happy
Show: Do Re Mi
Opened: December 1960
Lyrics by: Adolph Green & Betty
Comden

Never Never Land
Show: Peter Pan
Opened: October 1954
Lyrics by: Adolph Green & Betty
Comden

Papa, Won't You Dance with Me?
Show: High Button Shoes
Opened: October 1947
Lyrics by: Sammy Cahn

The Party's Over
Show: Bells are Ringing
Opened: November 1956
Lyrics by: Adolph Green & Betty
Comden

People
Show: Funny Girl
Opened: March 1964
Lyrics by: Bob Merrill

Say, Darling
Show: Say, Darling
Opened: April 1958
Lyrics by: Adolph Green & Betty
Comden

Small World
Show: Gypsy
Opened: May 1959
Lyrics by: Stephen Sondheim

Jule Styne (continued)
Something's Always Happening on the River
Show: Say, Darling
Opened: April 1958
Lyrics by: Adolph Green & Betty
Comden

Together
Show: Gypsy
Opened: May 1959
Lyrics by: Stephen Sondheim

You Are Woman
Show: Funny Girl
Opened: March 1964
Lyrics by: Bob Merrill

You'll Never Get Away from Me
Show: Gypsy
Opened: May 1959
Lyrics by: Stephen Sondheim

Kay Swift *(1897-1993)*
Fine and Dandy
Show: Fine and Dandy
Opened: September 1930
Lyrics by: Paul James

Harry Tierney *(1895-1965)*
Alice Blue Gown
Show: Irene
Opened: November 1919
Lyrics by: Joseph McCarthy

If You're In Love You'll Waltz
Show: Rio Rita
Opened: Febrary 1927
Lyrics by: Joseph McCarthy

Irene
Show: Irene
Opened: November 1919
Lyrics by: Joseph McCarthy

Harry Tierney (continued)
The Kinkajou
Show: Rio Rita
Opened: Febrary 1927
Lyrics by. Joseph McCarthy

Rio Rita
Show: Rio Rita
Opened: Febrary 1927
Lyrics by. Joseph McCarthy

Albert Von Tilzer *(1878-1956)*
Put Your Arms Around Me Honey
Show: Madame Sherry
Opened: August 1910
Lyrics by. Junie McCree

Kurt Weill *(1900-1950)*
The Ballad of Mack the Knife
Show: Three-Penny Opera
Opened: March 1954
Lyrics by. Marc Blitstein

Green-Up Time
Show: Lovelife
Opened: October 1948
Lyrics by. Alan Jay Lerner

Here I'll Stay
Show: Lovelife
Opened: October 1948
Lyrics by. Alan Jay Lerner

My Ship
Show: Lady in the Dark
Opened: January 1941
Lyrics by. Ira Gershwin

Saga of Jenny
Show: Lady in the Dark
Opened: January 1941
Lyrics by. Ira Gershwin

September Song
Show: Knickerbocker Holiday
Opened: October 1938
Lyrics by. Maxwell Anderson

Kurt Weill (continued)
Speak Low
Show: One Touch of Venus
Opened: October 1943
Lyrics by. Ogden Nash

Richard Whiting *(1891-1938)*
Eadie Was a Lady
Show: Take a Chance
Opened: Novermber 1932
Lyrics by. B.G. DeSylva

You're an Old Smoothie
Show: Take a Chance
Opened: Novermber 1932
Lyrics by. B.G. DeSylva

Meredith Willson *(1902-1984)*
Goodnight, My Someone
Show: Music Man
Opened: December 1957
Lyrics by. Meredith Willson

I Ain't Down Yet
Show: Insinkable Molly Brown
Opened: November 1960
Lyrics by. Meredith Willson

Lida Rose
Show: Music Man
Opened: December 1957
Lyrics by. Meredith Willson

Marian the Librarian
Show: Music Man
Opened: December 1957
Lyrics by. Meredith Willson

Rock Island
Show: Music Man
Opened: December 1957
Lyrics by. Meredith Willson

Seventy-Six Trombones
Show: Music Man
Opened: December 1957
Lyrics by. Meredith Willson

Meredith Willson (continued)

Till There Was You
Show: Music Man
Opened: December 1957
Lyrics by. Meredith Willson

Wells Fargo Wagon
Show: Music Man
Opened: December 1957
Lyrics by. Meredith Willson

Vincent Youmans *(1898-1946)*

Deep in My Heart
Show: Lollipop
Opened: January 1924
Lyrics by. Zelda Sears

Drums in My Heart
Show: Through the Years
Opened: January 1932
Lyrics by. Edward Heyman

Great Day
Show: Great Day!
Opened: October 1929
Lyrics by. Billy Rose and Edward Eliscu

Hallelujah
Show: Hit the Deck
Opened: April 1927
Lyrics by. Clifford Grey & Leo Robbins

I Know That You Know
Show: Oh, Please!
Opened: December 1926
Lyrics by. Anne Caldwell

I Want to Be Happy
Show: No, No, Nanette
Opened: September 1925
Lyrics by. Irving Caesar

More Than You Know
Show: Great Day!
Opened: October 1929
Lyrics by. Billy Rose and Edward Eliscu

Vincent Youmans (continued)

No, No, Nanette
Show: No, No, Nanette
Opened: September 1925
Lyrics by. Irving Caesar

Sometimes I'm Happy
Show: Hit the Deck
Opened: April 1927
Lyrics by. Clifford Grey & Leo Robbins

Tea for Two
Show: No, No, Nanette
Opened: September 1925
Lyrics by. Irving Caesar

Through the Years
Show: Through the Years
Opened: January 1932
Lyrics by. Edward Heyman

Time on My Hands
Show: Smiles
Opened: November 1930
Lyrics by. Harold Adamson & Mack Gordon

Without a Song
Show: Great Day!
Opened: October 1929
Lyrics by. Billy Rose and Edward Eliscu

Maurice Yvain *(1891-1965)*

My Man
Show: Ziegfeld Follies
Opened: June 1921
Lyrics by. Channing Pollock

Section Three

ℬ

Shows
(Alphabetically Listed)

BROADWAY'S

COMPOSERS

↑
JULE STYNE (left), with his favorite writers —
BETTY COMDEN and ADOLPH GREEN.

←
SIGMUND ROMBERG, creator of more music
for the theatre than any other composer.

RAY HENDERSON (right) wrote the music
for eight shows with B.G. 'Buddy'
DeSylva (left) and LEW BROWN (center).
↓

All American
Show opening: March 1962
Music by: Charles Strouse
Lyrics by: Lee Adams
  Once Upon a Time

Allegro
Show opening: October 1947
Music by: Richard Rodgers
Lyrics by: Oscar Hammerstein II
  A Fellow Needs a Girl
  TheGentleman is a Dope
  So Far
  You Are Never Away

America's Sweetheart
Show opening: February 1931
Music by: Richard Rodgers
Lyrics by: Lorenz Hart
  I've Got Five Dollars

Americana
Show opening: October 1932
Music by: Jay Gorney
Lyrics by: E.Y. Harburg
  Brother Can You Spare a Dime?

Andre Charlot's Revue of 1924
Show opening: January 1924
Music by: Philip Braham
Lyrics by: Douglas Furber
  Limehouse Blues
Music by: Eubie Blake
Lyrics by: Noble Sissle
  You Were Meant for Me

Annie
Show opening: April 1977
Music by: Charles Strouse
Lyrics by: Martin Charnin
  Tomorrow

Annie Get Your Gun
Show opening: May 1946
Music by: Irving Berlin
Lyrics by: Irving Berlin
  Anything You Can Do
  Doin' What Comes Natur'lly

Annie Get Your Gun (continued)
  The Girl That I Marry
  I Got Lost in His Arms
  I Got the Sun in the Morning
  I'm An Indian, Too
  My Defenses are Down
  There's No Business Like
    Show Business
  They Say It's Wonderful
  You Can't Get a Man with a Gun

Anything Goes
Show opening: November 1934
Music by: Cole Porter
Lyrics by: Cole Porter
  All Through the Night
  Anything Goes
  Blow, Gabriel, Blow
  I Get a Kick Out cf You
  You're the Top

As Thousands Cheer
Show opening: September 1933
Music by: Irving Berlin
Lyrics by: Irving Berlin
  Easter Parade
  Heat Wave
  Not for All the Rice in China

Babes in Arms
Show opening: April 1937
Music by: Richard Rodgers
Lyrics by: Lorenz Hart
  All at Once
  Johnny One Note
  I Wish I Were in Love Again
  TheLady is a Tramp
  My Funny Valentine
  Where or When

Babes in Toyland
Show opening: October 1903
Music by: Victor Herbert
Lyrics by: Glen MacDonough
  I Can't Do the Sum
  March of the Toys
  Toyland

Band Wagon
Show opening: June 1931
Music by: Arthur Schwartz
Lyrics by: Howard Dietz
   Dancing in the Dark
   I Love Louisa
   New Sun in the Sky

Bells are Ringing
Show opening: November 1956
Music by: Jule Styne
Lyrics by: Adoph Green & Betty Comden
   Just in Time
   TheParty's Over

Best Foot Forward
Show opening: October 1941
Music by: Hugh Martin
Lyrics by: Ralph Blane
   Buckle Down Winsocki
   What Do You Think I Am?

Betsy
Show opening: December 1926
Music by: Irving Berlin
Lyrics by: Irving Berlin
   Blue Skies

Between the Devil
Show opening: December 1937
Music by: Arthur Schwartz
Lyrics by: Howard Dietz
   I See Your Face Before Me

Big Boy
Show opening: January 1925
Music by: Joseph Meyer
Lyrics by: B.G. DeSylva
   If You Knew Susie
Music by: Ray Henderson
Lyrics by: Lew Brown
   It All Depends on You

Bitter Sweet
Show opening: November 1929
Music by: Noël Coward
Lyrics by: Noël Coward
   I'll See You Again
   Ziguener

Blackbirds of 1928
Show opening: May 1928
Music by: Jimmy McHugh
Lyrics by: Dorothy Fields
   Diga Diga Doo
   I Can't Give You Anything
   But Love

Bloomer Girl
Show opening: October 1944
Music by: Harold Arlen
Lyrics by: E.Y. Harburg
   The Eagle and Me
   Right as the Rain
   When the Boys Come Home

Blue Paradise
Show opening: August 1915
Music by: Sigmund Romberg
Lyrics by: Herbert Reynolds
   Aüf Wiedersehn

Bombo
Show opening: October 1921
Music by: Louis Silvers
Lyrics by: B.G. DeSylva
   April Showers

Boys from Syacuse
Show opening: November 1938
Music by: Richard Rodgers
Lyrics by: Lorenz Hart
   Falling in Love With Love
   Sing for Your Supper
   This Can't Be Love

Brigadoon

Show opening: March 1947
Music by: Frederick Loewe
Lyrics by: Alan Jay Lerner
   Almost Like Being in Love
   Come to Me, Bend to Me
   Heather on the Hill
   There But for You Go I

By Jupiter

Show opening: November 1938
Music by: Richard Rodgers
Lyrics by: Lorenz Hart
   Wait Till You See Her

Bye Bye Birdie

Show opening: April 1960
Music by: Charles Strouse
Lyrics by: Lee Adams
   Kids
   Put on a Happy Face
   A Lot of Livin' to Do

Cabaret

Show opening: November 1966
Music by: John Kander
Lyrics by: Fred Ebb
   Cabaret

Cabin in the Sky

Show opening: October 1940
Music by: Vernon Duke
Lyrics by: John Latouche
   Cabin in the Sky
Lyrics by: Ted Fetter
   Taking a Chance on Love

Call Me Madam

Show opening: October 1950
Music by: Irving Berlin
Lyrics by: Irving Berlin
   The Best Thing for You
   **The Hostess with the Mostes' on
      the Ball**
   It's a Lovely Day Today
   You're Just in Love

Call Me Mister

Show opening: April 1946
Music by: Harold Rome
Lyrics by: Harold Rome
   South America, Take It Away

Camelot

Show opening: December 1960
Music by: Frederick Loewe
Lyrics by: Alan Jay Lerner
   Camelot
   Follow Me
   How to Handle a Woman
   I Loved You Once in Silence
   If Ever I Would Leave You
   What Do the Simple Folk Do?

Can-Can

Show opening: May 1953
Music by: Cole Porter
Lyrics by: Cole Porter
   C'est Magnifique
   I Love Paris
   It's All Right with Me

Candide

Show opening: December 1956
Music by: Leonard Bernstein
Lyrics by: Richard Wilbur
   Make Our Garden Grow

Carnival

Show opening: April 1961
Music by: Bob Merrill
Lyrics by: Bob Merrill
   Love Makes the World Go Round

Carousel

Show opening: April 1945
Music by: Richard Rodgers
Lyrics by: Oscar Hammerstein II
   If I Loved You
   June is Bustin' Out All Over
   Mr. Snow
   A Real Nice Clambake
   What's the Use of Wond'rin'
   You'll Never Walk Alone
   Soliloquy (Carousel)

Cat and the Fiddle
Show opening: October 1931
Music by: Jerome Kern
Lyrics by: Otto Harbach
    The Night Was Made for Love
    She Didn't Say "Yes"

Cats
Show opening: October 1982
Music by: Andrew Lloyd Webber
Lyrics by: T.S. Eliot
    Memory

Chocolate Soldier
Show opening: September 1909
Music by: Oscar Straus
Lyrics by: Stanislaus Stange
    My Hero
    Sympathy

Chorus Line
Show opening: April 1975
Music by: Marvin Hamlisch
Lyrics by: Edward Kleban
    One
    What I Did for Love

Connecticut Yankee
Show opening: November 1927
Music by: Richard Rodgers
Lyrics by: Lorenz Hart
    My Heart Stood Still
    Thou Swell

Countess Maritza
Show opening: September 1926
Music by: Emmerich Kalman
Lyrics by: Harry Smith
    Play, Gypsies--Dance, Gypsies

Damn Yankees
Show opening: May 1955
Music by: Richard Adler
Lyrics by: Jerry Ross
    Heart
    Whatever Lola Wants

Desert Song
Show opening: November 1926
Music by: Sigmund Romberg
Lyrics by: Otto Harbach & Oscar
        Hammerstein II
    Desert Song
    One Alone
    Riff Song
    Romance

Do I Hear a Waltz?
Show opening: March 1965
Music by: Richard Rodgers
Lyrics by: Stephen Sondheim
    Do I Hear a Waltz?

Do Re Mi
Show opening: December 1960
Music by: Jule Styne
Lyrics by: Adolph Green & Betty Comden
    Cry Like the Wind
    Make Someone Happy

DuBarry Was a Lady
Show opening: December 1939
Music by: Cole Porter
Lyrics by: Cole Porter
    Do I Love You?
    Friendship
    Well, Did You Evah?

Earl Carroll Vanities
Show opening: August 1927
Music by: Ray Noble
Lyrics by: Peg Connelly
    Good Night, Sweetheart

Evita
Show opening: September 1979
Music by: Andrew Lloyd Webber
Lyrics by: Tim Rice
    Don't Cry for Me, Argentina

Face the Music
Show opening: February 1932
Music by: Irving Berlin
Lyrics by: Irving Berlin
> **Let's Have Another Cup o' Coffee**
> **Soft Lights and Sweet Music**

Fanny
Show opening: November 1954
Music by: Harold Rome
Lyrics by: Harold Rome
> **Fanny**

Fantasticks, The
Show opening: May 1960
Music by: Harvey Schmidt
Lyrics by: Tom Jones
> **Soon It's Gonna Rain**
> **Try to Remember**

Fiddler on the Roof
Show opening: September 1964
Music by: Jerry Bock
Lyrics by: Sheldon Harnick
> **If I Were a Rich Man**
> **Matchmaker, Matchmaker**
> **Miracle of Miracles**
> **Sunrise, Sunset**
> **To Life (L'Chaim)**
> **Tradition**

Fifty Miles from Boston
Show opening: February 1908
Music by: George M. Cohan
Lyrics by: George M. Cohan
> **Harrigan**

Fifty Million Frenchmen
Show opening: November 1929
Music by: Cole Porter
Lyrics by: Cole Porter
> **You Do Something to Me**

Fine and Dandy
Show opening: September 1930
Music by: Kay Swift
Lyrics by: Paul James
> **Fine and Dandy**

Finian's Rainbow
Show opening: January 1947
Music by: Burton Lane
Lyrics by: E.Y. Harburg
> **How Are Things in Glocca**
> **Morra?**
> **If This Isn't Love**
> **Look to the Rainbow**
> **Old Devil Moon**
> **That Great Come-and-Get-It**
> **Day**
> **When I'm Not Near the Girl**
> **I Love**

Fiorello!
Show opening: November 1959
Music by: Jerry Bock
Lyrics by: Sheldon Harnick
> **I Love a Cop**
> **Little Tin Box**
> **On the Side of the Angels**
> **Politics and Poker**
> **Til Tomorrow**

Firefly
Show opening: December 1912
Music by: Rudolf Friml
Lyrics by: Otto Hauerbach (Harbach)
> **Giannina Mia**
> **Love is Like a Firefly**
> **Sympathy**

Florodora
Show opening: November 1900`
Music by: Leslie Stuart
Lyrics by: Leslie Stuart
> **Tell Me Pretty Maiden**

Flower Drum Song
Show opening: December 1958
Music by: Richard Rodgers
Lyrics by: Oscar Hammerstein II
> **I Enjoy Being a Girl**
> **Love, Look Away**
> **You Are Beautiful**

Flying Colors
Show opening: September 1932
Music by: Arthur Schwartz
Lyrics by: Howard Dietz
Alone Together
Louisiana Hayride
A Shine on Your Shoes

Flying High
Show opening: March 1930
Music by: Ray Henderson
Lyrics by: B.G. DeSylva and Lew Brown
Thank Your Father

Follow Thru
Show opening: January 1929
Music by: Ray Henderson
Lyrics by: B.G. DeSylva and Lew Brown
Button Up Your Overcoat

Fortune Teller
Show opening: September 1928
Music by: Victor Herbert
Lyrics by: Harry B.Smith
Gypsy Love Song

Forty-Five Minutes from Broadway
Show opening: January 1906
Music by: George M. Cohan
Lyrics by: George M. Cohan
Forty-Five Minutes from Broadway
Mary's a Grand Old Name

Funny Face
Show opening: November 1927
Music by: George Gershwin
Lyrics by: Ira Gershwin
Funny Face
He Loves and She Loves
'S Wonderful

Funny Girl
Show opening: March 1964
Music by: Jule Styne
Lyrics by: Bob Merrill
Don't Rain on My Parade
People
You Are Woman

Funny Thing Happened on the Way to the Forum
Show opening: May 1962
Music by: Stephen Sondheim
Lyrics by: Stephen Sondheim
Comedy Tonight

Garrick Gaieties
Show opening: May 1925
Music by: Richard Rodgers
Lyrics by: Lorenz Hart
Manhattan
Mountain Greenery
Sentimental Me

Gay Divorce
Show opening: November 1932
Music by: Cole Porter
Lyrics by: Cole Porter
Night and Day

Gentlemen Prefer Blondes
Show opening: December 1949
Music by: Jule Styne
Lyrics by: Leo Robin
Bye, Bye, Baby
Diamonds Are a Girl's Best Friend

George Washington Jr.
Show opening: February 1906
Music by: George M. Cohan
Lyrics by: George M. Cohan
You're a Grand Old Flag

George White's Scandals (4th Edition)
Show opening: August 1922
Music by: George Gershwin
Lyrics by: B.G. DaSylva & Arthur Francis
(Ira Gershwin)
I'll Build a Stairway to Paradise

George White's Scandals (6th Edition)
Show opening: June 1924
Music by: George Gershwin
Lyrics by: B.G. DaSylva & Ballard Macdonald
Somebody Loves Me

George White's Scandals (8th Edition)
Show opening: June 1926
Music by: Ray Henderson
Lyrics by: B.G. DeSylva and Lew Brown
Birth of the Blues
Black Bottom
Rhapsody in Blue (Instrumental)

George White's Scandals (11th Edition)
Show opening: September 1931
Music by: Ray Henderson
Lyrics by: Lew Brown
Life is Just a Bowl of Cherries
My Song
That's Why Darkies Were Born
This is the Missus
The Thrill is Gone

Girl Crazy
Show opening: October 1930
Music by: George Gershwin
Lyrics by: Ira Gershwin
Bidin' My Time
But Not for Me
Could You Use Me?
Embraceable You
I Got Rythm
Treat Me Rough

Girl Friend, The
Show opening: March 1926
Music by: Richard Rodgers
Lyrics by: Lorenz Hart
The Blue Room
The Girl Friend

Girl from Utah
Show opening: August 1914
Music by: Jerome Kern
Lyrics by: Herbert Reynolds
They Didn't Believe Me

Girl of My Dreams
Show opening: August 1911
Music by: Karl Hoschna
Lyrics by: Otto Harbach
Girl of My Dreams

Godspell
Show opening: May 1971
Music by: Stephen Schwartz
Lyrics by: John-Michael Tebelak
Day by Day

Good News!
Show opening: September 1927
Music by: Ray Henderson
Lyrics by: B.G. DeSylva and Lew Brown
The Best Things in Life Are Free
Good News
Lucky in Love
Varsity Drag

Great Day!
Show opening: October 1929
Music by: Vincent Youmans
Lyrics by: Billy Rose and Edward Eliscu
Great Day
More Than You Know
Without a Song

Greenwich Village Follies (6th Edition)
Show opening: September 1924
Music by: Cole Porter
Lyrics by: Cole Porter
I'm in Love Again

Greenwillow
Show opening: March 1960
Music by: Frank Loesser
Lyrics by: Frank Loesser
Summertime Love

Guys and Dolls
Show opening: November 1950
Music by: Frank Loesser
Lyrics by: Frank Loesser
Bushel and a Peck
Guys and Dolls
I'll Know
If I Were a Bell
I've Never Been in Love Before
Luck Be a Lady
Sit Down You're Rockin' the Boa

Gypsy
Show opening: May 1959
Music by: Jule Styne
Lyrics by: Stephen Sondheim
  All I Need is the Girl
  Everything's Coming Up Roses
  Let Me Entertain You
  Little Lamb
  Small World
  Together
  You'll Never Get Away from Me

Hair
Show opening: April 1968
Music by: Galt MacDermot
Lyrics by: Gerome Ragni & James Rado
  Aquarius
  Let the Sunshine In

Hazel Flagg
Show opening: February 1953
Music by: Jule Styne
Lyrics by: Bob Hilliard
  How Do You Speak to an Angel?

Hello, Dolly!
Show opening: January 1964
Music by: Jerry Herman
Lyrics by: Jerry Herman
  Hello, Dolly!
  It Only Takes a Moment
  Ribbons Down My Back

High Button Shoes
Show opening: October 1947
Music by: Jule Styne
Lyrics by: Sammy Cahn
  I Still Get Jealous
  Papa, Won't You Dance with Me?

Higher and Higher
Show opening: April 1940
Music by: Richard Rodgers
Lyrics by: Lorenz Hart
  It Never Entered My Mind

Hit the Deck
Show opening: April 1927
Music by: Vincent Youmans
Lyrics by: Clifford Grey & Leo Robbins
  Hallelujah
  Sometimes I'm Happy

Hold Everything
Show opening: October 1928
Music by: Ray Henderson
Lyrics by: B.G. DeSylva and Lew Brown
  You're the Cream in My Coffee

Hold On to Your Hats
Show opening: September 1940
Music by: Burton Lane
Lyrics by: E.Y. Harburg
  There's a Great Day Coming
  Manana
  The World in My Arms

How to Succeed in Business Without Really Trying
Show opening: October 1961
Music by: Frank Loesser
Lyrics by: Frank Loesser
  Brotherhood of Man
  Company Way
  I Believe in You

I Can Get It For You Wholesale
Show opening: March 1962
Music by: Harold Rome
Lyrics by: Harold Rome
  Have I Told You Lately?

I Do! I Do!
Show opening: December 1966
Music by: Harvey Schmidt
Lyrics by: Tom Jones
  My Cup Runneth Over

I Married an Angel
Show opening: May 1938
Music by: Richard Rodgers
Lyrics by: Lorenz Hart
  I Married an Angel
  Spring is Here

I'd Rather Be Right
Show opening: November 1937
Music by: Richard Rodgers
Lyrics by: Lorenz Hart
    Have You Met Miss Jones?

Illya Darling
Show opening: April 1967
Music by: Manos Hadjidakis
Lyrics by: Joe Darion
    Never on Sunday

Inside U.S.A.
Show opening: April 1948
Music by: Arthur Schwartz
Lyrics by: Howard Dietz
    Rhode Island is Famous for You

Insinkable Molly Brown
Show opening: November 1960
Music by: Meredith Willson
Lyrics by: Meredith Willson
    I Ain't Down Yet

International Revue
Show opening: February 1930
Music by: Jimmy McHugh
Lyrics by: Dorothy Fields
    Exactly Like You
    On the Sunny Side of the Street

Irene
Show opening: November 1919
Music by: Harry Tierney
Lyrics by: Joseph McCarthy
    Alice Blue Gown
    Irene

Jesus Christ Superstar
Show opening: October 1971
Music by: Andrew Lloyd Webber
Lyrics by: Tim Rice
    I Don't Know How to Love Him
    Superstar

Jubilee
Show opening: October 1935
Music by: Cole Porter
Lyrics by: Cole Porter
    Begin the Beguine
    Just One of Those Things
    Why Shouldn't I?

Jumbo
Show opening: November 1935
Music by: Richard Rodgers
Lyrics by: Lorenz Hart
    Little Girl Blue
    The Most Beautiful Girl in the World
    My Romance

King and I
Show opening: March 1951
Music by: Richard Rodgers
Lyrics by: Oscar Hammerstein
    Getting to Know You
    Hello, Young Lovers
    I Have Dreamed
    I Whistle a Happy Tune
    Shall We Dance?
    Something Wonderful
    We Kiss in a Shadow

Kismet
Show opening: December 1953
Music by: Alexander Borodin
Lyrics by: Robert Wright & George Forrest
    And This is My Beloved
    Baubles, Bangles and Beads
    Stranger in Paradise

Kiss Me Kate
Show opening: December 1940
Music by: Cole Porter
Lyrics by: Cole Porter
    Always True to You in May Fashion
    Another Op'nin, Another Show
    Bianca
    Brush Up Your Shakespeare

Kiss Me Kate (continued)
- So in Love
- Too Darn Hot
- We Open in Venice
- Were Thine That Special Face
- Where is the Life That Late I Led?
- Why Can't You Behave?
- Wunderbar

Knickerbocker Holiday
Show opening: October 1938
Music by: Kurt Weill
Lyrics by: Maxwell Anderson
- September Song

La Cage Aux Folles
Show opening: August 1983
Music by: Jerry Herman
Lyrics by: Harvey Fierstein
- The Best of Times

Lady, Be Good!
Show opening: December 1924
Music by: George Gershwin
Lyrics by: Ira Gershwin
- Fascinating Rhythm
- Oh! Lady Be Good

Lady in the Dark
Show opening: January 1941
Music by: Kurt Weill
Lyrics by: Ira Gershwin
- My Ship
- Saga of Jenny

Leave It to Me
Show opening: November 1938
Music by: Cole Porter
Lyrics by: Cole Porter
- Get Out of Town
- My Heart Belongs to Daddy

Let's Face It!
Show opening: October 1941
Music by: Cole Porter
Lyrics by: Cole Porter
- Let's Not Talk About Love

Life Begins at 8:40
Show opening: August 1934
Music by: Harold Arlen
Lyrics by: E.Y. Harburg & Ira Gershwin
- Let's Take a Walk Around the Block
- You're a Builder-Upper

Little Johnny Jones
Show opening: November 1904
Music by: George M. Cohan
Lyrics by: George M. Cohan .
- Give My Regards to Broadway
- Yankee Doodle Boy

Little Me
Show opening: November 1962
Music by: Cy Coleman
Lyrics by: Carolyn Leigh
- Real Live Girl

Little Night Music, A
Show opening: February 1973
Music by: Stephen Sondheim
Lyrics by: Hugh Wheeler
- Send in the Clowns

Little Show
Show opening: April 1929
Music by: Arthur Schwartz
Lyrics by: Howard Dietz
- I Guess I'll Have to Change My Plans

Lollipop
Show opening: January 1924
Music by: Vincent Youmans
Lyrics by: Zelda Sears
- Deep in My Heart

Louisiana Purchase
Show opening: May 1940
Music by: Irving Berlin
Lyrics by: Irving Berlin
- Fools Fall in Love
- It's a Lovely Day Tomorrow
- You're Lonely and I'm Lonely

Lovelife
Show opening: October 1948
Music by: Kurt Weill
Lyrics by: Alan Jay Lerner
    Green-Up Time
    Here I'll Stay
    Here I'll Stay

Madame Sherry
Show opening: August 1910
Music by: Karl Hoschna
Lyrics by: Otto Harbach
    Every Little Movement
Music by: Albert Von Tilzer
Lyrics by: Junie McCree
    Put Your Arms Around Me Honey

Make Mine Manhattan
Show opening: January 1948
Music by: Richard Lewine
Lyrics by: Arnold Horwitt
    Saturday Night in Cental Park

Mame
Show opening: May 1966
Music by: Jerry Herman
Lyrics by: Jerry Herman
    If He Walked Into My Life
    Mame
    My Best Girl
    We Need a Little Christmas

Man of La Mancha
Show opening: November 1965
Music by: Jerry Leigh
Lyrics by: Joe Darion
    Man of La Mancha (I, Don Quixote)
    Impossible Dream (The Quest)

Maytime
Show opening: August 1917
Music by: Sigmund Romberg
Lyrics by: Rida Johnson Young
    Will You Remember?

Me and Juliet
Show opening: May 1953
Music by: Richard Rodgers
Lyrics by: Oscar Hammerstein II
    No Other Love

Merry Malones
Show opening: September 1927
Music by: George M. Cohan
Lyrics by: George M. Cohan
    Molly Malone

Mexican Hayride
Show opening: January 1944
Music by: Cole Porter
Lyrics by: Cole Porter
    I Love You

Michael Todd's Peep Show
Show opening: June 1950
Music by: Harold Rome
Lyrics by: Harold Rome
    Pocketful of Dreams

Milk and Honey
Show opening: October 1961
Music by: Jerry Herman
Lyrics by: Jerry Herman
    Milk and Honey
    Shalom

Miss Liberty
Show opening: July 1949
Music by: Irving Berlin
Lyrics by: Irving Berlin
    Let's Take an Old Fashioned Walk

Mlle. Modiste
Show opening: December 1905
Music by: Victor Herbert
Lyrics by: Henry Blossom
    I Want What I Want When I Want It
    Kiss Me Again

Most Happy Fella
Show opening: May 1956
Music by: Frank Loesser
Lyrics by: Frank Loesser
    Big "D"
    Standing on the Corner

Mr. Wonderful
Show opening: March 1956
Music by: Jerry Bock
Lyrics by: Sheldon Harnick
    Mr. Wonderful
    Too Close for Comfort

Music Box Revue
Show opening: October 1922
Music by: Irving Berlin
Lyrics by: Irving Berlin
    Lady of the Evening
    Say It with Music

Music in the Air
Show opening: November 1932
Music by: Jerome Kern
Lyrics by: Oscar Hammerstein II
    I've Told Every Little Star

Music in the Air
Show opening: November 1932
Music by: Jerome Kern
Lyrics by: Oscar Hammerstein II
    The Song is You

Music Man
Show opening: December 1957
Music by: Meredith Willson
Lyrics by: Meredith Willson
    Goodnight, My Someone
    Lida Rose
    Marian the Librarian
    Rock Island
    Seventy-Six Trombones
    Till There Was You
    Wells Fargo Wagon

My Fair Lady
Show opening: March 1956
Music by: Frederick Loewe
Lyrics by: Alan Jay Lerner
    Get Me to the Church on Time
    I Could Have Danced All Night
    I've Grown Accustomed to
      Her Face
    Just You Wait
    On the Street Where You Live
    Rain in Spain
    With a Little Bit of Luck
    Wouldn't It Be Loverly?

My Maryland
Show opening: September 1927
Music by: Sigmund Romberg
Lyrics by: Dorothy Donnelly
    Your Land and My Land

Naughty Marietta
Show opening: November 1910
Music by: Victor Herbert
Lyrics by: Rida Johnson Young
    Ah! Sweet Mystery of Life
    I'm Falling in Love with Someone
    'Neath the Southern Moon
    Tramp! Tramp! Tramp!

New Moon
Show opening: September 1928
Music by: Sigmund Romberg
Lyrics by: Oscar Hammerstein II
    One Kiss
    Lover, Come Back to Me
    Softly, As in a Morning Sunrise
    Stouthearted Men
    Wanting You

New Yorkers
Show opening: December 1930
Music by: Cole Porter
Lyrics by: Cole Porter
    Love for Sale

No, No, Nanette
Show opening: September 1925
Music by: Vincent Youmans
Lyrics by: Irving Caesar
  I Want to Be Happy
  No, No, Nanette
  Tea for Two

No Strings
Show opening: March 1962
Music by: Richard Rodgers
Lyrics by: Richard Rodgers
  Sweetest Sounds

Of Thee I Sing
Show opening: December 1931
Music by: George Gershwin
Lyrics by: Ira Gershwin
  Love is Sweeping the Country
  Who Cares?
  Wintergreen for President

Oh, Boy!
Show opening: February 1917
Music by: Jerome Kern
Lyrics by: P.G. Wodehouse
  Till the Clouds Roll By

Oh, Kay!
Show opening: November 1926
Music by: George Gershwin
Lyrics by: Ira Gershwin
  Clap Yo' Hands
  Maybe
  Someone to Watch Over Me

Oh, Please!
Show opening: December 1926
Music by: Vincent Youmans
Lyrics by: Anne Caldwell
  I Know That You Know

Oklahoma!
Show opening: March 1943
Music by: Richard Rodgers
Lyrics by: Oscar Hammerstein II
  All er Nothin'
  I Cain't Say No
  Kansas City

Oklahoma! (continued)
  Many a New Day
  Oh, What a Beautiful Mornin'
  Oklahoma
  Out of My Dreams
  People Will Say We're in Love
  Pore Jud
  **The Surrey With the Fringe
    on Top**

Oliver!
Show opening: January 1963
Music by: Lionel Bart
Lyrics by: Lionel Bart
  As Long As He Needs Me
  I'd Do Anything
  Where is Love?

On a Clear Day You Can See Forever
Show opening: October 1965
Music by: Burton Lane
Lyrics by: Alan Jay Lerner
  On a Clear Day
  **What Did I Have That I Don't
    Have?**

On the Town
Show opening: December 1944
Music by: Leonard Bernstein
Lyrics by: Adolph Green & Betty Comden
  Lonely Town
  New York, New York
  Some Other Time

On Your Toes
Show opening: April 1936
Music by: Richard Rodgers
Lyrics by: Lorenz Hart
  Quiet Night
  Slaughter on Tenth Avenue
  There's a Small Hotel

One Touch of Venus
Show opening: October 1943
Music by: Kurt Weill
Lyrics by: Ogden Nash
  Speak Low

Orange Blossoms
Show opening: September 1922
Music by: Victor Herbert
Lyrics by: B.G.DeSylva
Kiss in the Dark

Out of This World
Show opening: December 1950
Music by: Cole Porter
Lyrics by: Cole Porter
Use Your Imagination

Paint Your Wagon
Show opening: November 1951
Music by: Frederick Loewe
Lyrics by: Alan Jay Lerner
I Talk to the Trees
They Call the Wind Maria

Pajama Game
Show opening: May 1954
Music by: Richard Adler
Lyrics by: Jerry Ross
Hernando's Hideaway
Hey, There
Steam Heat

Pal Joey
Show opening: December 1940
Music by: Richard Rodgers
Lyrics by: Lorenz Hart
Bewitched, Bothered and
Bewildered
I Could Write a Book

Panama Hattie
Show opening: October 1940
Music by: Cole Porter
Lyrics by: Cole Porter
Let's Be Buddies

Paris
Show opening: October 1928
Music by: Cole Porter
Lyrics by: Cole Porter
Let's Do It

Peter Pan
Show opening: Octrober 1954
Music by: Mark Sharlap
Lyrics by: Carolyn Leigh
I Gotta Crow
Music by: Jule Styne
Lyrics by: Adolph Green &
                Betty Comden
Never Never Land

Phantom of the Opera
Show opening: January 1988
Music by: Andrew Lloyd Webber
Lyrics by: Charles Hart
Music of the Night

Pipe Dream
Show opening: November 1955
Music by: Richard Rodgers
Lyrics by: Oscar Hammerstein
All At Once You Love Her

Plain and Fancy
Show opening: January 1955
Music by: Albert Hague
Lyrics by: Arnold Horwitt
Young and Foolish

Porgy and Bess
Show opening: October 1935
Music by: George Gershwin
Lyrics by: Ira Gershwin
Bess, You is My Woman Now
I Got Plenty of Nothin'
I Loves You, Porgy
It Ain't Necessarily So
There's a Boat dat's Leavin'
Soon for New York
Lyrics by: DuBose Heyward
Summertime

Present Arms
Show opening: April 1928
Music by: Richard Rodgers
Lyrics by: Lorenz Hart
You Took Advantage of Me

Princess Pat
Show opening: September 1915
Music by: Victor Herbert
Lyrics by: Henry Blossom
Neopolitan Love Song

Promises, Promises
Show opening: December 1968
Music by: Burt Bacharach
Lyrics by: Hal David
I'll Never Fall in Love Again
Promises, Promises

Red, Hot and Blue!
Show opening: October 1936
Music by: Cole Porter
Lyrics by: Cole Porter
It's De-Lovely
Ridin' High

Red Mill
Show opening: September 1906
Music by: Victor Herbert
Lyrics by: Henry Blossom
Because You're You
Every Day is Ladies' Day with Me

Revenge with Music
Show opening: November 1934
Music by: Arthur Schwartz
Lyrics by: Howard Dietz
If There is Someone Lovelier
Than You
You and the Night and the Music

Rio Rita
Show opening: Febrary 1927
Music by: Harry Tierney
Lyrics by: Joseph McCarthy
If You're In Love You'll Waltz
The Kinkajou
Rio Rita

Roar of the Greasepaint--
The Smell of the Crowd
Show opening: May 1965
Music by: Anthony Newley
Lyrics by: Leslie Bricusse
Who Can I Turn To?
A Wonderful Day Like Today

Roberta
Show opening: November 1933
Music by: Jerome Kern
Lyrics by: Otto Harbach
Smoke Gets in Your Eyes
The Touch of Your Hand
Yesterdays
You're Devastating

Rosalie
Show opening: January 1928
Music by: George Gershwin
Lyrics by: Ira Gershwin
How Long Has This Been Going
On?

Rose-Marie
Show opening: September 1924
Music by: Rudolf Friml
Lyrics by: Otto Harbach & Oscar
         Hammerstein II
Indian Love Call
Rose-Marie
Totem Tom-Tom

Sally
Show opening: December 1920
Music by: Jerome Kern
Lyrics by: B.G. DeSylva
Look for the Silver Lining

Say, Darling
Show opening: April 1958
Music by: Jule Styne
Lyrics by: Adolph Green & Betty Comden
Say, Darling
Something's Always Happening
on the River

Seven Lively Arts
Show opening: December 1944
Music by: Cole Porter
Lyrics by: Cole Porter
    Ev'rytime We Say Goodbye

She Loves Me
Show opening: Aapril 1963
Music by: Jerry Bock
Lyrics by: Sheldon Harnick
    She Loves Me

Shenandoah
Show opening: January 1975
Music by: Gary Geld
Lyrics by: Peter Udell
    Freedom

Show Girl
Show opening: July 1929
Music by: George Gershwin
Lyrics by: Ira Gershwin
    Liza

Show is On
Show opening: December 1936
Music by: Hoagy Carmichael
Lyrics by: Stanley Adams
    Little Old Lady

Showboat
Show opening: December 1927
Music by: Jerome Kern
Lyrics by: Oscar Hammerstein II
    Can't Help Lovin' Dat Man
    Life Upon the Wicked Stage
    Make Believe
    Ol' Man River
    Why Do I Love You?
    You Are Love
Lyrics by: Oscar Hammerstein II &
        P.G. Wodehouse
    Bill

Shuffle Along
Show opening: May 1921
Music by: Eubie Blake
Lyrics by: Noble Sissle
    I'm Just Wild About Harry

Silk Stockings
Show opening: February 1955
Music by: Cole Porter
Lyrics by: Cole Porter
    That's All

Simple Simon
Show opening: February 1930
Music by: Richard Rodgers
Lyrics by: Lorenz Hart
    Ten Cents a Dance

Sinbad
Show opening: February 1918
Music by: B.G. (Buddy) DeSylva
Lyrics by: B.G. DeSylva
    Cloe
Music by: Jean Schwartz
Lyrics by: Sam Lewis & Joe Young
    Rock-a-Bye Your Baby With a
        Dixie Melody

Sing Out the News
Show opening: September 1928
Music by: Harold Rome
Lyrics by: Harold Rome
    F.D.R. Jones

Smiles
Show opening: November 1930
Music by: Vincent Youmans
Lyrics by: Harold Adamson & Mack
        Gordon
    Time on My Hands

Something for the Boys
Show opening: January 1943
Music by: Cole Porter
Lyrics by: Cole Porter
    Hey, Good Lookin'
    Something for the Boys

Song of Norway
Show opening: August 1944
Music by: Edvard Grieg
Lyrics by: Robert Wright & George
			Forrest
	Freddy and His Fiddle
	I Love You
	Midsummer's Eve
	Strange Music

Sound of Music
Show opening: November 1959
Music by: Richard Rodgers
Lyrics by: Oscar Hammerstein II
	Climb Ev'ry Mountain
	Do-Re-Mi
	Edelweiss
	Maria
	My Favorite Things
	Sixteen Going on Seventeen
	So Long, Farewell
	The Sound of Music

South Pacific
Show opening: April 1949
Music by: Richard Rodgers
Lyrics by: Oscar Hammerstein II
	Bali Ha'i
	Bloody Mary
	A Cockeyed Optimist
	Dîtes-Moi
	Happy Talk
	Honey Bun
	**I'm Gonna Wash That Man Right
		Out of My Hair**
	Some Enchanted Evening
	There is Nothin ' Like a Dame
	This Nearly Was Mine
	A Wonderful Guy
	You've Got to Be Carefully Taught
	Younger Than Springtime

Spring is Here
Show opening: March 1929
Music by: Richard Rodgers
Lyrics by: Lorenz Hart
	With a Song in My Hert

St. Louis Woman
Show opening: March 1946
Music by: Harold Arlen
Lyrics by: Johnny Mercer
	Come Rain or Come Shine

Stop the World -- I Want to Get Off
Show opening: October 1962
Music by: Anthony Newley
Lyrics by: Leslie Bricusse
	Gonna Build a Mountain
	Once in a Lifetime
	What Kind of Fool Am I?

Stop! Look! Listen!
Show opening: December 1915
Music by: Irving Berlin
Lyrics by: Irving Berlin
	I Love a Piano

Strike Me Pink
Show opening: March 1933
Music by: Ray Henderson
Lyrics by: Lew Brown
	Strike Me Pink

Strike Up the Band
Show opening: January 1930
Music by: George Gershwin
Lyrics by: Ira Gershwin
	Feeling I'm Falling
	I've Got A Crush on You
	Soon
	Strike Up the Band

Student Prince in Heidelberg
Show opening: December 1924
Music by: Sigmund Romberg
Lyrics by: Dorothy Donnelly
	Deep in My Heart, Dear
	Drinking Song
	Golden Days

Subways Are For Sleeping
Show opening: December 1961
Music by: Jule Styne
Lyrics by: Adolph Green & Betty Comden
Be a Santa
Comes Once in a Lifetime

Sunny
Show opening: September 1925
Music by: Jerome Kern
Lyrics by: Otto Harbach & Oscar
Hammerstein II
Sunny
Who?

Sweet Adeline
Show opening: September 1929
Music by: Jerome Kern
Lyrics by: Oscar Hammerstein II
Don't Ever Leave Me
Why Was I Born?

Sweet Charity
Show opening: January 1966
Music by: Cy Coleman
Lyrics by: Dorothy Fields
Big Spender
If My Friends Could See Me Now

Sweethearts
Show opening: September 1913
Music by: Victor Herbert
Lyrics by: Robert B.Smith
Sweethearts

Take a Chance
Show opening: Novermber 1932
Music by: Richard A. Whiting
Lyrics by: B.G. DeSylva
Eadie Was a Lady
You're an Old Smoothie

Take Me Along
Show opening: October 1959
Music by: Bob Merrill
Lyrics by: Bob Merrill
Take Me Along

This is the Army
Show opening: July 1942
Music by: Irving Berlin
Lyrics by: Irving Berlin
American Eagles
**I Left My Heart at the
StageDoor Canteen**
**This is the Army, Mr.
Jones**

Three Twins
Show opening: June 1908
Music by: Karl Hoschna
Lyrics by: Otto Harbach
Cuddle Up a Little Closer
Lovey Mine

Three's a Crowd
Show opening: October 1930
Music by: Arthur Schwartz
Lyrics by: Howard Dietz
**Something to Remember
You By**

Three-Penny Opera
Show opening: March 1954
Music by: Kurt Weill
Lyrics by: Marc Blitstein
**The Ballad of Mack the
Knife**

Through the Years
Show opening: January 1932
Music by: Vincent Youmans
Lyrics by: Edward Heyman
Drums in My Heart
Through the Years

Too Many Girls
Show opening: Ocatober 1939
Music by: Richard Rodgers
Lyrics by: Lorenz Hart
**I Didn't Know What Time
It Was**
**I Like to Recognize the
Tune**

Trip to Chinatown, A
Show opening: November 1891
Music by: Percy Gaunt
Lyrics by: Charles Harris
After the Ball
Lyrics by: Percy Gaunt
The Bowery

Up in Central Park
Show opening: January 1945
Music by: Sigmund Romberg
Lyrics by: Dorothy Fields
Close As Pages in a Book
It Doesn't Cost You Anything
to Dream

Vagabond King
Show opening: September 1925
Music by: Rudolf Friml
Lyrics by: Brian Hooker & W.H. Post
Only a Rose
Some Day
Song of the Vagabonds

Very Warm for May
Show opening: November 1939
Music by: Jerome Kern
Lyrics by: Oscar Hammerstein II
All in Fun
All the Things You Are

Wake Up and Dream
Show opening: December 1929
Music by: Cole Porter
Lyrics by: Cole Porter
What is This Thing Called Love?

Walk a Little Faster
Show opening: December 1932
Music by: Vernon Duke
Lyrics by: E.Y. Harburg
April in Paris

Watch Your Step
Show opening: December 1914
Music by: Irving Berlin
Lyrics by: Irving Berlin
Play a Simple Melody

West Side Story
Show opening: September 1957
Music by: Leonard Bernstein
Lyrics by: Stephen Sondheim
America
Cool
Gee, Officer Krupke
I Feel Pretty
Maria
Something's Coming
Somewhere
Tonight

What Makes Sammy Run?
Show opening: February 1964
Music by: Ervin Drake
Lyrics by: Ervin Drake
A Room Without Windows

Where's Charley?
Show opening: October 1948
Music by: Frank Loesser
Lyrics by: Frank Loesser
My Darling, My Darling
Once in Love with Amy

Whoopee
Show opening: December 1928
Music by: Walter Donaldson
Lyrics by: Gus Kahn
Love Me or Leave Me
Makin' Whoopee

Wildcat
Show opening: December 1960
Music by: Cy Coleman
Lyrics by: Carolyn Leigh
Hey, Look Me Over

Wish You Were Here
Show opening: June 1952
Music by: Harold Rome
Lyrics by: Harold Rome
Wish You Were Here

Wonderful Town
Show opening: February 1953
Music by: Leonard Bernstein
Lyrics by: Adolph Green & Betty Comden
   Ohio

Yip, Yip, Yaphank
Show opening: September 1918
Music by: Irving Berlin
Lyrics by: Irving Berlin
   A Pretty Girl is Like a Melody
   Mandy
   Oh, How I Hate to Get Up in
      the Morning

Yokel Boy
Show opening: July 1939
Music by: Sam Stept
Lyrics by: Lew Brown & Charles Tobias
   Comes Love

You Never Know
Show opening: September 1938
Music by: Cole Porter
Lyrics by: Cole Porter
   At Long Last Love

You Said It
Show opening: January 1931
Music by: Harold Arlen
Lyrics by: Jack Yellen
   Learn to Croon

Ziegfeld Follies of 1921
Show opening: June 1921
Music by: Maurice Yvain
Lyrics by: Channing Pollock
   My Man
Music by: James Hanley
Lyrics by: Grant Clarke
   Second Hand Rose

Ziegfeld Follies of 1922
Show opening: June 1922
Music by: Ed Gallagher
Lyrics by: Al Shean & Ernest Ball
   Mr. Gallagher and Mr. Shean
Music by: Ole Olsen
Lyrics by: Chic Johnson &
      Ernest Brewer
   Oh! Gee, Oh! Gosh, Oh!
   Golly, I'm in Love

Ziegfeld Follies of 1934
Show opening: January 1934
Music by: Vernon Duke
Lyrics by: E.Y. Harburg
   I Like the Likes of You
   What is There to Say?

Ziegfeld Follies of 1935
Show opening: January 1935
Music by: Vernon Duke
Lyrics by: E.Y. Harburg
   I Can't Get Started

Section Four

ᛟ

Chronological Openings
of the Shows
Listed in Section Three

BROADWAY'S LEADING COMPOSERS

←
VICTOR HERBERT, born in Ireland, was the first important composer of the American musical stage.

FRANK LOESSER began composing for films; switched to creating both words and music for the theatre.   →

JERRY BOCK (left), nearly always called upon the talents of gifted lyricist SHELDON HARNICK.
↓

1891

Show: **A Trip to Chinatown**
Composer: Percy Gaunt
Lyrics by: Charles Harris

1900

Show: **Florodora**
Composer: Leslie Stuart
Lyrics by: Leslie Stuart

1903

Show: **Babes in Toyland**
Composer: Victor Herbert
Lyrics by: Glen MacDonough

1904

Show: **Little Johnny Jones**
Composer: George M. Cohan
Lyrics by: George M. Cohan .

1905

Show: **Mlle. Modiste**
Composer: Victor Herbert
Lyrics by: Henry Blossom

Show: **Forty-Five Minutes from Broadway**
Composer: George M. Cohan
Lyrics by: George M. Cohan

1906

Show: **George Washington Jr.**
Composer: George M. Cohan
Lyrics by: George M. Cohan

Show: **Red Mill**
Composer: Victor Herbert
Lyrics by: Henry Blossom

1908

Show: **Fifty Miles from Boston**
Composer: George M. Cohan
Lyrics by: George M. Cohan

1908

Show: **Three Twins**
Composer: Karl Hoschna
Lyrics by: Otto Harbach

1909

Show: **Chocolate Soldier**
Composer: Oscar Straus
Lyrics by: Stanislaus Stange

1910

Show: **Madame Sherry**
Composer: Albert Von Tilzer
& Karl Hoschna
Lyrics by: Junie McCree & Otto Harbach

Show: **Naughty Marietta**
Composer: Victor Herbert
Lyrics by: Rida Johnson Young

1911

Show: **Girl of My Dreams**
Composer: Karl Hoschna
Lyrics by: Otto Harbach

1912

Show: **Firefly**
Composer: Rudolf Friml
Lyrics by: Otto Hauerbach (Harbach)

1913

Show: **Sweethearts**
Composer: Victor Herbert
Lyrics by: Robert B.Smith

1914

Show: **Girl from Utah**
Composer: Jerome Kern
Lyrics by: Herbert Reynolds

Show: **Watch Your Step**
Composer: Irving Berlin
Lyrics by: Irving Berlin

1915

Show: **Blue Paradise**
Composer: Sigmund Romberg
Lyrics by: Herbert Reynolds

Show: **Princess Pat**
Composer: Victor Herbert
Lyrics by: Henry Blossom

Show: **Stop! Look! Listen!**
Composer: Irving Berlin
Lyrics by: Irving Berlin

1917

Show: **Oh, Boy!**
Composer: Jerome Kern
Lyrics by: P.G. Wodehouse

1917 (continued)
Show: **Maytime**
Composer: Sigmund Romberg
Lyrics by: Rida Johnson Young

1918

Show: **Sinbad**
Composer: B.G. (Buddy)
DeSylva & Jean Schwartz
Lyrics by: B.G. DeSylva
Sam Lewis & Joe Young

Show: **Yip, Yip, Yaphank**
Composer: Irving Berlin
Lyrics by: Irving Berlin

1919

Show: **Irene**
Composer: Harry Tierney
Lyrics by: Joseph McCarthy

1920

Show: **Sally**
Composer: Jerome Kern
Lyrics by: B.G. DeSylva

1921

Show: **Bombo**
Composer: Louis Silvers
Lyrics by: B.G. DeSylva

Show: **Shuffle Along**
Composer: Eubie Blake
Lyrics by: Noble Sissle

Show: **Ziegfeld Follies**
Composer: Maurice Yvain &
James Hanley
Lyrics by: Channing Pollock &
Grant Clarke

1922

Show: **George White's
Scandals (4th Edition)**
Composer: George Gershwin
Lyrics by: B.G. DeSylva & Arthur
Francis (Ira Gershwin)

Show: **Music Box Revue**
Composer: Irving Berlin
Lyrics by: Irving Berlin

1922 (continued)
Show: **Orange Blossoms**
Composer: Victor Herbert
Lyrics by: B.G.DeSylva

Show: **Ziegfeld Follies of 1922**
Composer: Ed Gallagher & Ole
Olsen
Lyrics by: Al Shean, Ernest Ball,
Chic Johnson & Ernest
Brewer

1924

Show: **Andre Charlot's Revue
of 1924**
Composer: Philip Braham &
Eubie Blake
Lyrics by: Douglas Furber &
Noble Sissle

Show: **George White's
Scandals (6th Edition)**
Composer: George Gershwin
Lyrics by: B.G. DeSylva &
Ballard Macdonald

Show: **Greenwich Village
Follies (6th Edition)**
Composer: Cole Porter
Lyrics by: Cole Porter

Show: **Lady, Be Good!**
Composer: George Gershwin
Lyrics by: Ira Gershwin

Show: **Lollipop**
Composer: Vincent Youmans
Lyrics by: Zelda Sears

Show: **Rose-Marie**
Composer: Rudolf Friml
Lyrics by: Otto Harbach & Oscar
Hammerstein II

Show: **Student Prince in
Heidelberg**
Composer: Sigmund Romberg
Lyrics by: Dorothy Donnelly

1925

Show: **Big Boy**
Composer: Joseph Meyer &
 Ray Henderson
Lyrics by: B.G. DeSylva.& Lew
 Brown

Show: **Garrick Gaieties**
Composer: Richard Rodgers
Lyrics by: Lorenz Hart

Show: **No, No, Nanette**
Composer: Vincent Youmans
Lyrics by: Irving Caesar

Show: **Sunny**
Composer: Jerome Kern
Lyrics by: Otto Harbach & Oscar
 Hammerstein II

Show: **Vagabond King**
Composer: Rudolf Friml
Lyrics by: Brian Hooker & W.H.
 Post

1926

Show: **Betsy**
Composer: Irving Berlin
Lyrics by: Irving Berlin

Show: **Countess Maritza**
Composer: Emmerich Kalman
Lyrics by: Harry Smith

Show: **Desert Song**
Composer: Sigmund Romberg
Lyrics by: Otto Harbach & Oscar
 Hammerstein II

Show: **Garrick Gaieties**
Composer: Richard Rodgers
Lyrics by: Lorenz Hart

Show: **George White's
 Scandals (8th Edition)**
Composer: Ray Henderson
Lyrics by: B.G. DeSylva and
 Lew Brown

1926 (continued)

Show: **Oh, Kay!**
Composer: George Gershwin
Lyrics by: Ira Gershwin

Show: **Oh, Please!**
Composer: Vincent Youmans
Lyrics by: Anne Caldwell

Show: **The Girl Friend**
Composer: Richard Rodgers
Lyrics by: Lorenz Hart

1927

Show: **Connecticut Yankee**
Composer: Richard Rodgers
Lyrics by: Lorenz Hart

Show: **Earl Carroll Vanities**
Composer: Ray Noble
Lyrics by: Peg Connelly

Show: **Funny Face**
Composer: George Gershwin
Lyrics by: Ira Gershwin

Show: **Good News!**
Composer: Ray Henderson
Lyrics by: B.G. DeSylva and
 Lew Brown

Show: **Hit the Deck**
Composer: Vincent Youmans
Lyrics by: Clifford Grey & Leo
 Robbins

Show: **Merry Malones**
Composer: George M. Cohan
Lyrics by: George M. Cohan

Show: **My Maryland**
Composer: Sigmund Romberg
Lyrics by: Dorothy Donnelly

<u>1927</u> (continued)

Show: **Rio Rita**
Composer: Harry Tierney
Lyrics by: Joseph McCarthy

Show: **Showboat**
Composer: Jerome Kern
Lyrics by: Oscar Hammerstein II
             & P.G. Wodehouse

<u>1928</u>

Show: **Blackbirds of 1928**
Composer: Jimmy McHugh
Lyrics by: Dorothy Fields

Show: **Fortune Teller**
Composer: Victor Herbert
Lyrics by: Harry B.Smith

Show: **Hold Everything**
Composer: Ray Henderson
Lyrics by: B.G. DeSylva and
             Lew Brown

Show: **New Moon**
Composer: Sigmund Romberg
Lyrics by: Oscar Hammerstein II

Show: **Paris**
Composer: Cole Porter
Lyrics by: Cole Porter

Show: **Present Arms**
Composer: Richard Rodgers
Lyrics by: Lorenz Hart

Show: **Rosalie**
Composer: George Gershwin
Lyrics by: Ira Gershwin

Show: **Sing Out the News**
Composer: Harold Rome
Lyrics by: Harold Rome

Show: **Strike Up the Band**
Composer: George Gershwin
Lyrics by: Ira Gershwin

<u>1928</u> (continued)

Show: **Whoopee**
Composer: Walter Donaldson
Lyrics by: Gus Kahn

<u>1929</u>

Show: **Bitter Sweet**
Composer: Noël Coward
Lyrics by: Noël Coward

Show: **Fifty Million Frenchmen**
Composer: Cole Porter
Lyrics by: Cole Porter

Show: **Follow Thru**
Composer: Ray Henderson
Lyrics by: B.G. DeSylva and
             Lew Brown

Show: **Great Day!**
Composer: Vincent Youmans
Lyrics by: Billy Rose and
             Edward Eliscu

Show: **Little Show**
Composer: Arthur Schwartz
Lyrics by: Howard Dietz

Show: **Show Girl**
Composer: George Gershwin
Lyrics by: Ira Gershwin

Show: **Spring is Here**
Composer: Richard Rodgers
Lyrics by: Lorenz Hart

Show: **Sweet Adeline**
Composer: Jerome Kern
Lyrics by: Oscar Hammerstein II

Show: **Wake Up and Dream**
Composer: Cole Porter
Lyrics by: Cole Porter

<u>1930</u>

Show: **Fine and Dandy**
Composer: Kay Swift
Lyrics by: Paul James

<u>1930</u> (continued)

Show: **Flying High**
Composer: Ray Henderson
Lyrics by: B.G. DeSylva and
Lew Brown

Show: **Girl Crazy**
Composer: George Gershwin
Lyrics by: Ira Gershwin

Show: **International Revue**
Composer: Jimmy McHugh
Lyrics by: Dorothy Fields

Show: **New Yorkers**
Composer: Cole Porter
Lyrics by: Cole Porter

Show: **Simple Simon**
Composer: Richard Rodgers
Lyrics by: Lorenz Hart

Show: **Smiles**
Composer: Vincent Youmans
Lyrics by: Harold Adamson &
Mack Gordon

Show: **Strike Up the Band**
Composer: George Gershwin
Lyrics by: Ira Gershwin

Show: **Three's a Crowd**
Composer: Arthur Schwartz
Lyrics by: Howard Dietz

<u>1931</u>

Show: **America's Sweetheart**
Composer: Richard Rodgers
Lyrics by: Lorenz Hart

Show: **Band Wagon**
Composer: Arthur Schwartz
Lyrics by: Howard Dietz

Show: **Cat and the Fiddle**
Composer: Jerome Kern
Lyrics by: Otto Harbach

<u>1931</u> (continued)

Show: **George White's**
Scandals (11th Edition)
Composer: Ray Henderson
Lyrics by: Lew Brown

Show: **Of Thee I Sing**
Composer: George Gershwin
Lyrics by: Ira Gershwin

Show: **You Said It**
Composer: Harold Arlen
Lyrics by: Jack Yellen

<u>1932</u>

Show: **Americana**
Composer: Jay Gorney
Lyrics by: E.Y. Harburg

Show: **Face the Music**
Composer: Irving Berlin
Lyrics by: Irving Berlin

Show: **Flying Colors**
Composer: Arthur Schwartz
Lyrics by: Howard Dietz

Show: **Gay Divorce**
Composer: Cole Porter
Lyrics by: Cole Porter

Show: **Music in the Air**
Composer: Jerome Kern
Lyrics by: Oscar Hammerstein II

Show: **Take a Chance**
Composer: Richard A. Whiting
Lyrics by: B.G. DeSylva

Show: **Through the Years**
Composer: Vincent Youmans
Lyrics by: Edward Heyman

Show: **Walk a Little Faster**
Composer: Vernon Duke
Lyrics by: E.Y. Harburg

<u>1933</u>

Show: **As Thousands Cheer**
Composer: Irving Berlin
Lyrics by: Irving Berlin

1933 (continued)

Show: **Roberta**
Composer: Jerome Kern
Lyrics by: Otto Harbach

Show: **Strike Me Pink**
Composer: Ray Henderson
Lyrics by: Lew Brown

1934

Show: **Anything Goes**
Composer: Cole Porter
Lyrics by: Cole Porter

Show: **Life Begins at 8:40**
Composer: Harold Arlen
Lyrics by: E.Y. Harburg & Ira
          Gershwin

Show: **Revenge with Music**
Composer: Arthur Schwartz
Lyrics by: Howard Dietz

Show: **Ziegfeld Follies**
Composer: Vernon Duke
Lyrics by: E.Y. Harburg

1935

Show: **Jubilee**
Composer: Cole Porter
Lyrics by: Cole Porter

Show: **Jumbo**
Composer: Richard Rodgers
Lyrics by: Lorenz Hart

Show: **Porgy and Bess**
Composer: George Gershwin
Lyrics by: Ira Gershwin

Show: **Ziegfeld Follies**
Composer: Vernon Duke
Lyrics by: E.Y. Harburg

1936

Show: **On Your Toes**
Composer: Richard Rodgers
Lyrics by: Lorenz Hart

Show: **Red, Hot and Blue!**
Composer: Cole Porter
Lyrics by: Cole Porter

1936 (continued)

Show: **Show is On**
Composer: Hoagy Carmichael
Lyrics by: Stanley Adams

1937

Show: **Babes in Arms**
Composer: Richard Rodgers
Lyrics by: Lorenz Hart

Show: **Between the Devil**
Composer: Arthur Schwartz
Lyrics by: Howard Dietz

Show: **I'd Rather Be Right**
Composer: Richard Rodgers
Lyrics by: Lorenz Hart

1938

Show: **Boys from Syacuse**
Composer: Richard Rodgers
Lyrics by: Lorenz Hart

Show: **By Jupiter**
Composer: Richard Rodgers
Lyrics by: Lorenz Hart

Show: **I Married an Angel**
Composer: Richard Rodgers
Lyrics by: Lorenz Hart

Show: **Knickerbocker Holiday**
Composer: Kurt Weill
Lyrics by: Maxwell Anderson

Show: **Leave It to Me**
Composer: Cole Porter
Lyrics by: Cole Porter

Show: **You Never Know**
Composer: Cole Porter
Lyrics by: Cole Porter

1939

Show: **DuBarry Was a Lady**
Composer: Cole Porter
Lyrics by: Cole Porter

Show: **Too Many Girls**
Composer: Richard Rodgers
Lyrics by: Lorenz Hart

1939 (continued)

Show: **Very Warm for May**
Composer: Jerome Kern
Lyrics by: Oscar Hammerstein II

Show: **Yokel Boy**
Composer: Sam Stept
Lyrics by: Lew Brown & Charles Tobias

1940

Show: **Cabin in the Sky**
Composer: Vernon Duke
Lyrics by: John Latouche

Show: **Higher and Higher**
Composer: Richard Rodgers
Lyrics by: Lorenz Hart

Show: **Hold On to Your Hats**
Composer: Burton Lane
Lyrics by: E.Y. Harburg

Show: **Kiss Me Kate**
Composer: Cole Porter
Lyrics by: Cole Porter

Show: **Louisiana Purchase**
Composer: Irving Berlin
Lyrics by: Irving Berlin

Show: **Pal Joey**
Composer: Richard Rodgers
Lyrics by: Lorenz Hart

Show: **Panama Hattie**
Composer: Cole Porter
Lyrics by: Cole Porter

1941

Show: **Best Foot Forward**
Composer: Hugh Martin
Lyrics by: Ralph Blane

Show: **Lady in the Dark**
Composer: Kurt Weill
Lyrics by: Ira Gershwin

Show: **Let's Face It!**
Composer: Cole Porter
Lyrics by: Cole Porter

1942

Show: **This is the Army**
Composer: Irving Berlin
Lyrics by: Irving Berlin

1943

Show: **Oklahoma!**
Composer: Richard Rodgers
Lyrics by: Oscar Hammerstein

Show: **One Touch of Venus**
Composer: Kurt Weill
Lyrics by: Ogden Nash

Show: **Something for the Boys**
Composer: Cole Porter
Lyrics by: Cole Porter

1944

Show: **Bloomer Girl**
Composer: Harold Arlen
Lyrics by: E.Y. Harburg

Show: **Mexican Hayride**
Composer: Cole Porter
Lyrics by: Cole Porter

Show: **On the Town**
Composer: Leonard Bernstein
Lyrics by: Adolph Green & Betty Comden

Show: **Seven Lively Arts**
Composer: Cole Porter
Lyrics by: Cole Porter

Show: **Song of Norway**
Composer: Edvard Grieg
Lyrics by: Robert Wright & George Forrest

1945

Show: **Carousel**
Composer: Richard Rodgers
Lyrics by: Oscar Hammerstein

Show: **Up in Central Park**
Composer: Sigmund Romberg
Lyrics by: Dorothy Fields

<u>**1946**</u>

Show: **Annie Get Your Gun**
Composer: Irving Berlin
Lyrics by: Irving Berlin

Show: **Call Me Mister**
Composer: Harold Rome
Lyrics by: Harold Rome

Show: **St. Louis Woman**
Composer: Harold Arlen
Lyrics by: Johnny Mercer

<u>**1947**</u>

Show: **Allegro**
Composer: Richard Rodgers
Lyrics by: Oscar Hammerstein

Show: **Brigadoon**
Composer: Frederick Loewe
Lyrics by: Alan Jay Lerner

Show: **Finian's Rainbow**
Composer: Burton Lane
Lyrics by: E.Y. Harburg

Show: **High Button Shoes**
Composer: Jule Styne
Lyrics by: Sammy Cahn

<u>**1948**</u>

Show: **Inside U.S.A.**
Composer: Arthur Schwartz
Lyrics by: Howard Dietz

Show: **Lovelife**
Composer: Kurt Weill
Lyrics by: Alan Jay Lerner

Show: **Make Mine Manhattan**
Composer: Richard Lewine
Lyrics by: Arnold Horwitt

Show: **Where's Charley?**
Composer: Frank Loesser
Lyrics by: Frank Loesser

<u>**1949**</u>

Show: **Gentlemen Prefer Blondes**
Composer: Jule Styne
Lyrics by: Leo Robin

<u>**1949**</u> (continued)

Show: **Miss Liberty**
Composer: Irving Berlin
Lyrics by: Irving Berlin

Show: **South Pacific**
Composer: Richard Rodgers
Lyrics by: Oscar Hammerstein II

<u>**1950**</u>

Show: **Call Me Madam**
Composer: Irving Berlin
Lyrics by: Irving Berlin

Show: **Guys and Dolls**
Composer: Frank Loesser
Lyrics by: Frank Loesser

Show: **Michael Todd's Peep Show**
Composer: Harold Rome
Lyrics by: Harold Rome

Show: **Out of This World**
Composer: Cole Porter
Lyrics by: Cole Porter

<u>**1951**</u>

Show: **King and I**
Composer: Richard Rodgers
Lyrics by: Oscar Hammerstein

Show: **Paint Your Wagon**
Composer: Frederick Loewe
Lyrics by: Alan Jay Lerner

<u>**1952**</u>

Show: **Wish You Were Here**
Composer: Harold Rome
Lyrics by: Harold Rome

<u>**1953**</u>

Show: **Can-Can**
Composer: Cole Porter
Lyrics by: Cole Porter

Show: **Hazel Flagg**
Composer: Jule Styne
Lyrics by: Bob Hilliard

1953 (continued)

Show: **Kismet**
Composer: Alexander Borodin
Lyrics by: Robert Wright &
George Forrest

Show: **Me and Juliet**
Composer: Richard Rodgers
Lyrics by: Oscar Hammerstein

Show: **Wonderful Town**
Composer: Leonard Bernstein
Lyrics by: Adolph Green & Betty
Comden

1954

Show: **Fanny**
Composer: Harold Rome
Lyrics by: Harold Rome

Show: **Pajama Game**
Composer: Richard Adler
Lyrics by: Jerry Ross

Show: **Peter Pan**
Composer: Jule Styne
Lyrics by: Adolph Green & Betty
Comden

Show: **Three-Penny Opera**
Composer: Kurt Weill
Lyrics by: Marc Blitstein

1955

Show: **Damn Yankees**
Composer: Richard Adler
Lyrics by: Jerry Ross

Show: **Pipe Dream**
Composer: Richard Rodgers
Lyrics by: Oscar Hammerstein II

Show: **Plain and Fancy**
Composer: Albert Hague
Lyrics by: Arnold Horwitt

Show: **Silk Stockings**
Composer: Cole Porter
Lyrics by: Cole Porter

1956

Show: **Bells are Ringing**
Composer: Jule Styne
Lyrics by: Adoph Green & Betty
Comden

Show: **Candide**
Composer: Leonard Bernstein
Lyrics by: Richard Wilbur

Show: **Most Happy Fella**
Composer: Frank Loesser
Lyrics by: Frank Loesser

Show: **Mr. Wonderful**
Composer: Jerry Bock
Lyrics by: Sheldon Harnick

Show: **My Fair Lady**
Composer: Frederick Loewe
Lyrics by: Alan Jay Lerner

1957

Show: **Music Man**
Composer: Meredith Willson
Lyrics by: Meredith Willson

Show: **West Side Story**
Composer: Leonard Bernstein
Lyrics by: Stephen Sondheim

1958

Show: **Flower Drum Song**
Composer: Richard Rodgers
Lyrics by: Oscar Hammerstein

Show: **Say, Darling**
Composer: Jule Styne
Lyrics by: Adolph Green & Betty
Comden

1959

Show: **Fiorello!**
Composer: Jerry Bock
Lyrics by: Sheldon Harnick

Show: **Gypsy**
Composer: Jule Styne
Lyrics by: Stephen Sondheim

1959 (continued)
> *Show:* **Sound of Music**
> *Composer:* Richard Rodgers
> *Lyrics by:* Oscar Hammerstein II

> *Show:* **Take Me Along**
> *Composer:* Bob Merrill
> *Lyrics by:* Bob Merrill

1960
> *Show:* **Bye Bye Birdie**
> *Composer:* Charles Strouse
> *Lyrics by:* Lee Adams

> *Show:* **Camelot**
> *Composer:* Frederick Loewe
> *Lyrics by:* Alan Jay Lerner

> *Show:* **Do Re Mi**
> *Composer:* Jule Styne
> *Lyrics by:* Adolph Green & Betty
>   Comden

> *Show:* **Fantasticks**
> *Composer:* Harvey Schmidt
> *Lyrics by:* Tom Jones

> *Show:* **Greenwillow**
> *Composer:* Frank Loesser
> *Lyrics by:* Frank Loesser

> *Show:* **Unsinkable Molly Brown**
> *Composer:* Meredith Willson
> *Lyrics by:* Meredith Willson

> *Show:* **Wildcat**
> *Composer:* Cy Coleman
> *Lyrics by:* Carolyn Leigh

1961
> *Show:* **Carnival**
> *Composer:* Bob Merrill
> *Lyrics by:* Bob Merrill

> *Show:* **How to Succeed in**
>   **Business Without**
>   **Really Trying**
> *Composer:* Frank Loesser
> *Lyrics by:* Frank Loesser

1961 (continued)
> *Show:* **Milk and Honey**
> *Composer:* Jerry Herman
> *Lyrics by:* Jerry Herman

> *Show:* **Subways Are For**
>   **Sleeping**
> *Composer:* Jule Styne
> *Lyrics by:* Adolph Green & Betty
>   Comden

1962
> *Show:* **All American**
> *Composer:* Charles Strouse
> *Lyrics by:* Lee Adams

> *Show:* **Funny Thing Happened**
>   **on the Way to the Forum**
> *Composer:* Stephen Sondheim
> *Lyrics by:* Stephen Sondheim

> *Show:* **I Can Get It For You**
>   **Wholesale**
> *Composer:* Harold Rome
> *Lyrics by:* Harold Rome

> *Show:* **Little Me**
> *Composer:* Cy Coleman
> *Lyrics by:* Carolyn Leigh

> *Show:* **No Strings**
> *Composer:* Richard Rodgers
> *Lyrics by:* Richard Rodgers

> *Show:* **Stop the World --**
>   **I Want to Get Off**
> *Composer:* Anthony Newley
> *Lyrics by:* Leslie Bricusse

1963
> *Show:* **Oliver!**
> *Composer:* Lionel Bart
> *Lyrics by:* Lionel Bart

> *Show:* **She Loves Me**
> *Composer:* Jerry Bock
> *Lyrics by:* Sheldon Harnick

1964

Show: **Fiddler on the Roof**
Composer: Jerry Bock
Lyrics by: Sheldon Harnick

Show: **Funny Girl**
Composer: Jule Styne
Lyrics by: Bob Merrill

Show: **Hello, Dolly!**
Composer: Jerry Herman
Lyrics by: Jerry Herman

Show: **What Makes Sammy Run?**
Composer: Ervin Drake
Lyrics by: Ervin Drake

1965

Show: **Do I Hear a Waltz?**
Composer: Richard Rodgers
Lyrics by: Stephen Sondheim

Show: **Man of La Mancha**
Composer: Jerry Leigh
Lyrics by: Joe Darion

Show: **On a Clear Day You Can See Forever**
Composer: Burton Lane
Lyrics by: Alan Jay Lerner

Show: **Roar of the Greasepaint-- The Smell of the Crowd**
Composer: Anthony Newley
Lyrics by: Leslie Bricusse

1966

Show: **Cabaret**
Composer: John Kander
Lyrics by: Fred Ebb

Show: **I Do! I Do!**
Composer: Harvey Schmidt
Lyrics by: Tom Jones

Show: **Mame**
Composer: Jerry Herman
Lyrics by: Jerry Herman

1966 (continued)

Show: **Sweet Charity**
Composer: Cy Coleman
Lyrics by: Dorothy Fields

1967

Show: **Illya Darling**
Composer: Manos Hadjidakis
Lyrics by: Joe Darion

1968

Show: **Hair**
Composer: Galt MacDermot
Lyrics by: Gerome Ragni & James Rado

Show: **Promises, Promises**
Composer: Burt Bacharach
Lyrics by: Hal David

1971

Show: **Godspell**
Composer: Stephen Schwartz
Lyrics by: John-Michael Tebelak

Show: **Jesus Christ Superstar**
Composer: Andrew Lloyd Webber
Lyrics by: Tim Rice

1973

Show: **A Little Night Music**
Composer: Stephen Sondheim
Lyrics by: Hugh Wheeler

1975

Show: **Chorus Line**
Composer: Marvin Hamlisch
Lyrics by: Edward Kleban

Show: **Shenandoah**
Composer: Gary Geld
Lyrics by: Peter Udell

1977

Show: **Annie**
Composer: Charles Strouse
Lyrics by: Martin Charnin

1979

Show: **Evita**
Composer: Andrew Lloyd Webber
Lyrics by: Tim Rice

1982

Show: **Cats**
Composer: Andrew Lloyd Webber
Lyrics by: T.S. Eliot

1983

Show: **La Cage Aux Folles**
Composer: Jerry Herman
Lyrics by: Harvey Fierstein

1988

Show: **Phantom of the Opera**
Composer: Andrew Lloyd Webber
Lyrics by: Charles Hart

Appendix

Ø

Memorable Movie Melodies
by Broadway's Composers
(Alphabetically Listed)

Ac-cent-tchu-ate the Positive
Movie: Here Come the Waves (1944)
Composer: Harold Arlen
Lyricist: Johnny Mercer

All at Once
Movie: Where Do We Go From
        Here? (1945)
Composer: Kurt Weill
Lyricist: Ira Gershwin

All I Owe Ioway
Movie: State Fair (1945)
Composer: Richard Rodgers
Lyricist: Oscar Hammerstein II

All Through the Day
Movie: Centennial Summer (1946)
Composer: Jerome Kern
Lyricist: Oscar Hammerstein II

Anywhere I Wander
Movie: Hans Christian Andersen
        (1951)
Composer: Frank Loesser
Lyricist: Frank Loesser

Baby, It's Cold Outside
Movie: Neptune's Daughter (1949)
Composer: Frank Loesser
Lyricist: Frank Loesser

Be a Clown
Movie: The Pirate (1948)
Composer: Cole Porter
Lyricist: Cole Porter

Better Luck Next Time
Movie: Easter Parade (1948)
Composer: Irving Berlin
Lyricist: Irving Berlin

Blue Moon
Movie: Hollywood Revue of 1933
Composer: Richard Rodgers
Lyricist: Lorenz Hart

Blues in the Night
Movie: Blues in the Night (1941)
Composer: Harold Arlen
Lyricist: Johnny Mercer

Bojangles of Harlem
Movie: Swing Time (1936)
Composer: Jerome Kern
Lyricist: Dorothy Fields

The Boy Next Door
Movie: Meet Me in St. Louis (1944)
Composer: Hugh Martin
Lyricist: Ralph Blaine

Californ-i-ay
Movie: Can't Help Singing (1944)
Composer: Jerome Kern
Lyricist: E.Y. Harburg

Can I Forget You
Movie: High, Wide and Handsome
        (1937)
Composer: Jerome Kern
Lyricist: Oscar Hammerstein II

Can't Help Singing
Movie: Can't Help Singing (1944)
Composer: Jerome Kern
Lyricist: E.Y. Harburg

Carioca
Movie: Flying Down to Rio (1933)
Composer: Vincent Youmans
Lyricist: Edward Eliscu & Gus Kahn

Change Partners
Movie: Carefree (1938)
Composer: Irving Berlin
Lyricist: Irving Berlin

Cheek to Cheek
Movie: Top Hat (1935)
Composer: Irving Berlin
Lyricist: Irving Berlin

A Couple of Swells
Movie: Easter Parade (1948)
Composer: Irving Berlin
Lyricist: Irving Berlin

Dearly Beloved
Movie: You Were Never Lovelier
(1942)
Composer: Jerome Kern
Lyricist: Johnny Mercer

Delishious
Movie: Delicious (1931)
Composer: George Gershwin
Lyricist: Ira Gershwin

Ding Dong! The Witch is Dead
Movie: Ther Wizard of Oz (1939)
Composer: Harold Arlen
Lyricist: E.Y Harburg

The Donkey Serenade
Movie: The Firefly (1937)
Composer: Rudolf Friml
Lyricist: Robert Wright & George
Forrest

Don't Fence Me In
Movie: Hollywood Canteen (1944)
Composer: Cole Porter
Lyricist: Cole Porter

Easy to Love
Movie: Born to Dance (1936)
Composer: Cole Porter
Lyricist: Cole Porter

Everything I Have is Yours
Movie: Dancing Lady (1933)
Composer: Burton Lane
Lyricist: Harold Adamson

A Fine Romance
Movie: Swing Time (1936)
Composer: Jerome Kern
Lyricist: Dorothy Fields

Flying Down to Rio
Movie: Flying Down to Rio (1933)
Composer: Vincent Youmans
Lyricist: Edward Eliscu & Gus Kahn

A Foggy Day (in London Town)
Movie: A Damsel in Distress (1937)
Composer: George Gershwin
Lyricist: Ira Gershwin

The Folks Who Live on the Hill
Movie: High, Wide and Handsome
(1937)
Composer: Jerome Kern
Lyricist: Oscar Hammerstein II

For You, For Me, For Evermore
Movie: The Shocking Miss Pilgrim
(1946)
Composer: George Gershwin
Lyricist: Ira Gershwin

Get Thee Behind Me Satan
Movie: Follow the Fleet (1936)
Composer: Irving Berlin
Lyricist: Irving Berlin

Gigi
Movie: Gigi (1958)
Composer: Frederick Loewe
Lyricist: Alan Jay Lerner

Halleluyah, I'm a Bum
Movie: Halleluyah, I'm a Bum (1933)
Composer: Richard Rodgers
Lyricist: Lorenz Hart

Happiness is Thing Called Joe
Movie: Cabin in the Sky (1943)
Composer: Harold Arlen
Lyricist: E.Y. Harburg

**Have Yourself a Merry Little
Christmas**
Movie: Meet Me in St. Louis (1944)
Composer: Hugh Martin
Lyricist: Ralph Blane

Hey, Babe, Hey
Movie: Born to Dance (1936)
Composer: Cole Porter
Lyricist: Cole Porter

Hit the Road to Dreamland
Movie: Star Spangled Rhythm (1942)
Composer: Harold Arlen
Lyricist: Johnny Mercer

Hooray for Love
Movie: Casbah (1948)
Composer: Harold Arlen
Lyricist: Leo Robin

How About You
Movie: Babes on Broadway (1941)
Composer: Burton Lane
Lyricist: Ralph Freed

How Can You Believe Me When
I Said I Loved You
Movie: Royal Wedding (1951)
Composer: Burton Lane
Lyricist: Alan Jay Lerner

How Sweet You Are
Movie: Thank Your Lucky Stars
    (1943)
Composer: Arthur Schwartz
Lyricist: Frank Loesser

I Concentrate on You
Movie: Broadway Melody of 1940
Composer: Cole Porter
Lyricist: Cole Porter

I Don't Want to Walk Without You
Movie: Sweater Girl (1942)
Composer: Jule Styne
Lyricist: Frank Loesser

I Dream Too Much
Movie: I Dream Too Much (1935)
Composer: Jerome Kern
Lyricist: Dorothy Fields

I Feel a Song Coming On
Movie: Every Night at Eight (1935)
Composer: Jimmy McHugh
Lyricist: Dorothy Fields & George

I Was Doing All Right
Movie: Goldwyn Follies (1938)
Composer: George Gershwin
Lyricist: Ira Gershwin

I Won't Dance
Movie: Roberta (1935)
Composer: Jerome Kern
Lyricist: Dorothy Fields, Oscar
        Hammerstein II, Otto Harbach
        & Jimmy McHugh

If I Had a Talking Picture of You
Movie: Sunny Side Up (1929)
Composer: Ray Henderson
Lyricist: B.G. De Sylva & Lew Brown

If I Only Had a Brain
Movie: The Wizard of Oz (1939)
Composer: Harold Arlen
Lyricist: E.Y. Harburg

I'll Walk Alone
Movie: Follow the Boys (1944)
Composer: Jule Styne
Lyricist: Sammy Cahn

I'm A Dreamer (Aren't We All)
Movie: Sunny Side Up (1929)
Composer: Ray Henderson
Lyricist: B.G. DeSylva & Lew Brown

I'm Glad I'm Not Young Anymore
Movie: Gigi (1958)
Composer: Frederick Loewe
Lyricist: Alan Jay Lerner

I'm in the Mood for Love
Movie: Every Night at Eight (1935)
Composer: Jimmy McHugh
Lyricist: Dorothy Fields

I'm Old Fashioned
Movie: You Were Never Lovelier
    (1942)
Composer: Jerome Kern
Lyricist: Johnny Mercer

I'm Putting All My Eggs in One Basket
Movie: Follow the Fleet (1936)
Composer: Irving Berlin
Lyricist: Irving Berlin

In the Still of the Night
Movie: Rosalie (1937)
Composer: Cole Porter
Lyricist: Cole Porter

Inchworm
Movie: Hans Christian Andersen (1951)
Composer: Frank Loesser
Lyricist: Frank Loesser

Isn't It Kinda Fun
Movie: State Fair (1945)
Composer: Richard Rodgers
Lyricist: Oscar Hammerstein II

Isn't It Romantic
Movie: Love Me Tonight (1932)
Composer: Richard Rodgers
Lyricist: Lorenz Hart

Isn't This A Lovely Day
Movie: Top Hat (1935)
Composer: Irving Berlin
Lyricist: Irving Berlin

It Might As Well Be Spring
Movie: State Fair (1945)
Composer: Richard Rodgers
Lyricist: Oscar Hammerstein II

It's A Grand Night for Singing
Movie: State Fair (1945)
Composer: Richard Rodgers
Lyricist: Oscar Hammerstein II

It's a Most Unusual Day
Movie: A Date with Judy (1948)
Composer: Jimmy McHugh
Lyricist: Harold Adamson

It's Easy to Remember
Movie: Mississippi (1935)
Composer: Richard Rodgers
Lyricist: Lorenz Hart

It's Magic
Movie: Romance on the High Seas (1948)
Composer: Jule Styne
Lyricist: Sammy Kahn

It's Only a Paper Moon
Movie: Take a Chance (1933)
Composer: Harold Arlen
Lyricist: E.Y. Harburg & Billy Rose

I've Got My Eyes on You
Movie: Broadway Melody of 1940
Composer: Cole Porter
Lyricist: Cole Porter

I've Got My Love to Keep Me Warm
Movie: On the Avenue (1937)
Composer: Irving Berlin
Lyricist: Irving Berlin

I've Got You Under My Skin
Movie: Born to Dance (1936)
Composer: Cole Porter
Lyricist: Cole Porter

The Lady's in Love with You
Movie: Some Like It Hot (1939)
Composer: Burton Lane
Lyricist: Frank Loesser

The Last Time I Saw Paris
Movie: Lady, Be Good (1941)
Composer: Jerome Kern
Lyricist: Oscar Hammerstein II

Let Yourself Go
Movie: Follow the Fleet (1936)
Composer: Irving Berlin
Lyricist: Irving Berlin

Let's Call the Whole Thing Off
Movie: Shall We Dance (1937)
Composer: George Gershwin
Lyricist: Ira Gershwin

Let's Face the Music and Dance
Movie: Follow the Fleet (1936)
Composer: Irving Berlin
Lyricist: Irving Berlin

Let's Fall in Love
Movie: Let's Fall in Love (1934)
Composer: Harold Arlen
Lyricist: Ted Koehler

Let's Take the Long Way Home
Movie: Here Come the Waves (1944)
Composer: Harold Arlen
Lyricist: Johnny Mercer

Long Ago and Far Away
Movie: Cover Girl (1944)
Composer: Jerome Kern
Lyricist: Ira Gershwin

Love is Here to Stay
Movie: Goldwyn Follies (1938)
Composer: George Gershwin
Lyricist: Ira Gershwin

Love of My Life
Movie: The Pirate (1948)
Composer: Cole Porter
Lyricist: Cole Porter

Love Walked In
Movie: Goldwyn Follies (1938)
Composer: George Gershwin
Lyricist: Ira Gershwin

Lovely to Look At
Movie: Roberta (1935)
Composer: Jerome Kern
Lyricist: Dorothy Fields & Jimmy McHugh

A Lovely Way to Spend an Evening
Movie: Higher and Higher (1943)
Composer: Jimmy McHugh
Lyricist: Harold Adamson

Lover
Movie: Love Me Tonight (1932)
Composer: Richard Rodgers
Lyricist: Lorenz Hart

The Man That Got Away
Movie: A Star is Born (1954)
Composer: Harold Arlen
Lyricist: Ira Gershwin

Mimi
Movie: Love Me Tonight (1932)
Composer: Richard Rodgers
Lyricist: Lorenz Hart

More and More
Movie: Can't Help Singing (1944)
Composer: Jerome Kern
Lyricist: E.Y. Harburg

My Girl Back Home
Movie: South Pacific (1958)
Composer: Richard Ridgers
Lyricist: Oscar Hammerstein II

My Shining Hour
Movie: The Sky's the Limit (1943)
Composer: Harold Arlen
Lyricist: Johnny Mercer

Never Gonna Dance
Movie: Swing Time (1936)
Composer: Jerome Kern
Lyricist: Dorothy Fields

Nice Work If You Can Get It
Movie: A Damsel in Distress (1937)
Composer: George Gershwin
Lyricist: Ira Gershwin

The Night is Young
Movie: The Night is Young (1935)
Composer: Sigmund Romberg
Lyricist: Oscar Hammerstein II

**The Night They Invented
        Champagne**
Movie: Gigi (1958)
Composer: Frederick Loewe
Lyricist: Alan Jay Lerner

No Two People
Movie: Hans Christian Andersen
        (1951)
Composer: Frank Loesser
Lyricist: Frank Loesser

Now I Know
Movie: Up in Arms (1944)
Composer: Harold Arlen
Lyricist: Ted Koehler

One for My Baby
Movie: The Sky's the Limit (1943)
Composer: Harold Arlen
Lyricist: Johnny Mercer

Orchids in the Moonlight
Movie: Flying Down to Rio (1933)
Composer: Vincent Youmans
Lyricist: Edward Eliscu & Gus Kahn

Out of This World
Movie: Out of This World (1945)
Composer: Harold Arlen
Lyricist: Johnny Mercer

Over the Rainbow
Movie: The Wizard of Oz (1939)
Composer: Harold Arlen
Lyricist: E.Y. Harburg

The Piccolino
Movie: Top Hat (1935)
Composer: Irving Berlin
Lyricist: Irving Berlin

Pick Yourself Up
Movie: Swing Time (1936)
Composer: Jerome Kern
Lyricist: Dorothy Fields

Puttin' on the Ritz
Movie: Puttin' on the Ritz (1929)
Composer: Irving Berlin
Lyricist: Irving Berlin

Rosalie
Movie: Rosalie (1937)
Composer: Cole Porter
Lyricist: Cole Porter

Seal It with a Kiss
Movie: That Girl from Paris (1936)
Composer: Arthur Schwartz
Lyricist: Edward Hayman

Slap That Bass
Movie: Shall We Dance (1937)
Composer: George Gershwin
Lyricist: Ira Gershwin

Slumming on Park Avenue
Movie: On the Avenue (1937)
Composer: Irving Berlin
Lyricist: Irving Berlin

Something's Got to Give
Movie: Daddy Long Legs (1955)
Composer: Johnny Mercer
Lyricist: Johnny Mercer

Sonny Boy
Movie: The Singing Fool
Composer: Ray Henderson
Lyricist: B.G. DeSylva, Lew Brown
        & Al Jolson

Soon
Movie: Mississippi (1935)
Composer: Richard Rodgers
Lyricist: Lorenz Hart

Spring Will Be a Little Late This Year
Movie: Chirstmas Holiday (1944)
Composer: Frank Loesser
Lyricist: Frank Loesser

Steppin' Out with My Baby
Movie: Easter Parade (1948)
Composer: Irving Berlin
Lyricist: Irving Berlin

Sunny Side Up
Movie: Sunny Side Up (1929)
Composer: Ray Henderson
Lyricist: B.G. DeSylva & Lew Brown

Thank Heaven for Little Girls
Movie: Gifi (1958)
Composer: Frederick Loewe
Lyricist: Alan Jay Lerner

Thank You for A Lovely Evening
Movie: Have a Heart (1934)
Composer: Jimmy McHugh
Lyricist: Dorothy Fields

That Old Black Magic
Movie: Star Spangled Rhythm (1942)
Composer: Harold Arlen
Lyricist: Johnny Mercer

That's Entertainment
Movie: The Band Wagon (1953)
Composer: Arthur Schwartz
Lyricist: Howard Dietz

That's for Me
Movie: State Fair (1945)
Composer: Richard Rodgers
Lyricist: Oscar Hammerstein II

They All Laughed
Movie: Shall We Dance (1937)
Composer: George Gershwin
Lyricist: Ira Gershwin

They Can't Take That Away from Me
Movie: Shall We Dance (1937)
Composer: George Gershwin
Lyricist: Ira Gershwin

They're Either Too Young or Too Old
Movie: Thank Your Lucky Stars (1943)
Composer: Arthur Schwartz
Lyricist: Frank Loesser

This Time the Dream's on Me
Movie: Blues in the Night (1941)
Composer: Harold Arlen
Lyricist: Johnny Mercer

Three Coins in the Fountain
Movie: Three Coins in the Fountain (1954)
Composer: Jule Styne
Lyricist: Sammy Cahn

Thumbelina
Movie: Hans Christian Andersen (1951)
Composer: Frank Loesser
Lyricist: Frank Loesser

Top Hat, White Tie and Tails
Movie: Top Hat (1935)
Composer: Irving Berlin
Lyricist: Irving Berlin

The Trolley Song
Movie: Meet Me in St. Louis (1944)
Composer: Hugh Martin
Lyricist: Ralph Blane

True Love
Movie: High Society (1956)
Composer: Cole Porter
Lyricist: Cole Porter

Turn on the Heat
Movie: Sunny Side Up (1929)
Composer: Ray Henderson
Lyricist: B.G. DeSylva & Lew Brown

The Way You Look Tonight
Movie: Swing Time (1936)
Composer: Jerome Kern
Lyricist: Dorothy Field

We Saw the Sea
Movie: Follow the Fleet (1936)
Composer: Irving Berlin
Lyricist: Irving Berlin

We're Off to See the Wizard
Movie: The Wizard of Oz (1939)
Composer: Harold Arlen
Lyricist: E.Y. Harburg

When I Grow Too Old to Dream
Movie: The Night is Young (1935)
Composer: Sigmund Romberg
Lyricist: Oscar Hammerstein II

White Christmas
Movie: Holiday Inn (1942)
Composer: Irving Berlin
Lyricist: Irving Berlin

Wishing (Will Make It So)
Movie: Love Affair (1939)
Composer: B.G. DeSylva
Lyricist: B.G. DeSylva

A Woman in Love
Movie: Guys and Dolls (1955)
Composer: Frank Loesser
Lyricist: Frank Loesser

Wonderful Copenhagen
Movie: Hans Christian Andersen
       (1951)
Composer: Frank Loesser
Lyricist: Frank Loesser

You Are Too Beautiful
Movie: Hallelujah I'm a Bum, (1933)
Composer: Richard Rodgers
Lyricist: Lorenz Hart

You Couldn't Be Cuter
Movie: The Joy of Living (1938)
Composer: Jerome Kern
Lyricist: Dorothy Fields

You Were Never Lovelier
Movie: You Were Never Lovelier
       (1942)
Composer: Jerome Kern
Lyricist: Johnny Mercer

You'd Be So Nice to Come
      Home To
Movie: Something to Shout About
       (1942)
Composer: Cole Porter
Lyricist: Cole Porter

You're a Sweetheart
Movie: You're A Sweetheart (1937)
Composer: Jimmy McHugh
Lyricist: Harold Adamson

You're Nearer
Movie: Too Many Girls (1940)
Composer: Richard Rodgers
Lyricist: Lorenz Hart